RETURN TO GLORY

LSU'S CHAMPIONSHIP SEASON

The Times-Picayune

SP
SPORTS PUBLISHING
L.L.C.

www.sportspublishingllc.com

STAFF PHOTO BY ALEX BRANDON

The Times-Picayune

EDITORS

DAVID MEEKS
Sports editor
RICHARD RUSSELL
Sunday editor

DESIGN

GRANT STAUBLIN

COPY EDITORS

MICHAEL MONTALBANO
PHIL WEHRLE

PHOTO EDITOR

DOUG PARKER

DIGITAL IMAGING

G. ANDREW BOYD
GINA CLAUSI

RESEARCH

BRENT HIGHTOWER

Special thanks to Jim Amoss,
David Francis, Dan Shea,
George Berke and Crawford
Carroll

SPORTS PUBLISHING LLC

PUBLISHER

PETER L. BANNON

SENIOR MANAGING EDITORS

SUSAN M. MOYER
JOSEPH J. BANNON JR.

COORDINATING EDITOR

NOAH A. AMSTADTER

ART DIRECTOR

K. JEFFREY HIGGERSON

STAFF PHOTO BY ALEX BRANDON

STAFF PHOTO BY ALEX BRANDON

In the third quarter of the Sugar Bowl, LSU defensive end Marcus Spears, right, scored on an interception return to give the Tigers a 21-7 lead over Oklahoma.

STAFF PHOTO
BY ELIOT KAMENITZ

TIGERS FOLLOW SABAN'S VISION TO THE TOP

Years from now, when fans and pundits look back on LSU's 2003 national championship season, they'll talk about everything that went right for the Tigers on their way to the title.

But LSU's return to glory didn't start in the fall of 2003. Nothing worthwhile ever comes that fast or easy.

It started in 1999, when LSU Chancellor Mark Emmert decided Nick Saban, a defensive genius and masterful recruiter, was his personal choice to restore Tiger tradition.

It started when Saban saw LSU as a place with the potential for greatness, a sleeping giant where he could instill his philosophy of leadership, discipline and a commitment to academics. A place where he could build a champion.

It started when the state's oustanding high school players, long regarded as among the best in the nation, listened to Saban's pitch and decided to stay home, to build a legacy right here in Louisiana.

It started when they all came together and went to work. The 2003 season is more than one season. It's the culmination of hours, days and years of persistence, dedication and believing in each other.

"We started out this year saying we might not have the leadership we need and challenged everybody to be responsible for their own self-determination," Saban said. "And I have never seen a group of players that were able to do that and become so close and unified in the way they did it. They believed in themselves, they believed in each other. ... I'm telling you that's why we won the national championship, because of the character and ability of these guys and the attitude they played with. And I'm very proud of them."

It's a pride felt across Louisiana and in the hearts of Tigers fans everywhere. — David Meeks

LSU
49

UL-MONROE
7

Wide receiver Michael Clayton showed why he's LSU's No. 1 target Aug. 30, with two touchdowns against overmatched UL-Monroe.

CROWD PLEASER

LSU WIDE RECEIVER MICHAEL CLAYTON IS DAZZLING IN SEASON-OPENING WIN

It never rains at Tiger Stadium, right? Well, on this night it did, and the teams left the field because of severe weather. But the Tigers stormed past the Indians when they returned.

STAFF PHOTO BY ALEX BRANDON

LSU	49
ULM	7

TIGERS RECOVER FROM SLOW START, WEATHER DELAY

BY MIKE TRIPLETT STAFF WRITER

LSU should add a Michael Clayton surcharge to the cost of its football tickets. The junior receiver was definitely worth the price of admission in the Tigers' season opener.

Clayton caught six passes for 152 yards — including two dazzling touchdowns — to lead the Tigers to a 49-7 victory over Louisiana-Monroe to start the 2003 campaign.

Clayton, who during the preseason the LSU coaches also considered as a possible safety on defense, didn't play on defense on this night. But he was still the top crowd-pleaser on a night that tested the mettle of thousands of brave Tigers fans. The game was halted for 39 minutes due to severe weather early in the first quarter.

For a while, the game was just as sloppy as the weather.

LSU quarterback Matt Mauck didn't complete a pass in the first 11 minutes, and neither team scored in the first 23 minutes.

"I just think mentally we were flat in the beginning," LSU coach Nick Saban said. "I'm not sure the delay helped us. But we came around. And there were some things to be pleased about. We need to play not like we played at the beginning, but more like we played as the game went on."

STAFF PHOTO BY ALEX BRANDON

Running back Shyrone Carey and the Tigers left the Indians down-and-out in their opening act. After a sluggish first quarter on offense, LSU finished with 168 yards on the ground.

Eventually the Tigers broke the game open against their overmatched in-state foes. And with less than 20 seconds remaining in the first half, Mauck hooked up with Clayton on a 40-yard touchdown pass, giving LSU a 21-0 lead at the break.

Clayton caught the pass around the 25-yard line and shook his lone defender — who dove helplessly in the wrong direction — as he cruised toward the end zone.

Late in the third quarter, Clayton took another short pass, this one from backup quarterback Marcus Randall, and turned it into a 66-yard score. This time, Clayton ran the final 60 yards and made two defenders look helpless along the way. He finished with 169 total yards, also a career high, and matched a career best with his two touchdowns.

"It was fun to watch him a couple times," Mauck said. "We definitely have a lot of skill guys that can make some plays. I think tonight was a glimpse of what we can do. Obviously we can execute a little better."

Mauck wasn't quite as sharp out of the gate and did not develop a rhythm until midway through the second quarter.

The junior quarterback, playing for the first time since a season-ending foot injury against Florida in the 2002 season, passed for just 10 yards in the first quarter and threw an interception in the end zone early in the second quarter.

But he heated up soon after. The Tigers took advantage of terrific field position throughout the second quarter, starting their next four drives inside the 50-yard line.

LSU took advantage three times. Mauck threw an 8-yard touchdown pass to Devery Henderson, a 17-yard touchdown pass to Joseph Addai and the 40-yarder to Clayton — all within seven minutes.

Mauck left in the third quarter after completing 13 of 28 passes for 153 yards with one interception. Randall was 5-of-7 for 153 yards with one touchdown and no interceptions.

Even on an off night, LSU's offense demonstrated its big-strike ability.

"Matt and Marcus did a great job of getting us the ball, and Addai opened it up for us," Clayton said.

Addai was strong in his debut as LSU's starting tail-back. The sophomore carried 15 times for 81 yards, including eight for 56 in the first quarter.

"I think I played well. I did make some mistakes," Addai said, sharing the attitude of most of his teammates. "We just couldn't get things really, really going like we wanted to. But we just kept on playing hard."

Even Clayton dropped a couple of passes, both he and Saban pointed out.

Addai's backups, junior Shyrone Carey and freshman Alley Broussard, each scored on 1-yard runs in the second half.

Senior safety Jack Hunt scored the Tigers' other touchdown on a 31-yard interception return in the third quarter.

LSU's starting defense showed a sign of things to come. ULM's only touchdown came in the fourth quarter against the Tigers' second unit.

"I thought we played great. We gave up some points there at the end, but we had the (second team) in there, and they didn't do that bad," said Hunt, who said his first career touchdown was a thrill.

"Ever since I started playing football, I've always imagined myself making big plays. I guess I'll keep imagining it."

AP TOP 10

1. OKLAHOMA
2. OHIO STATE
3. MIAMI (FLA.)
4. SOUTHERN CAL
5. MICHIGAN
6. TEXAS
7. KANSAS STATE
8. GEORGIA
9. VIRGINIA TECH
10. PITTSBURGH
13. LSU

Preseason rankings

	1	2	3	4	
UL-MONROE	0	0	0	7	7
LSU	0	21	21	7	49

SCORING SUMMARY

LSU Devery Henderson 8-yard pass from Matt Mauck (Ryan Gaudet kick). Three plays, 24 yards in 1:11

LSU Joseph Addai 17-yard pass from Mauck (Gaudet kick). One play, 17 yards in 8 seconds

LSU Michael Clayton 40-yard pass from Mauck (Gaudet kick). Two plays, 30 yards in 33 seconds

LSU Shyrone Carey 1-yard run (Gaudet kick). 10 plays, 80 yards in 3:47

LSU Jack Hunt 31-yard return on interception (Chris Jackson kick)

LSU Clayton 66-yard pass from Marcus Randall (Jackson kick). Three plays, 80 yards in 1:02

UL-MONROE Kevin Payne 12-yard run (Tyler Kuecker kick). Eight plays, 73 yards in 3:28

LSU Alley Broussard 1-yard run (Jackson kick). Seven plays, 67 yards in 3:19

TEAM STATISTICS

CATEGORY	ULM	LSU
FIRST DOWNS	11	23
RUSHES-YARDS (NET)	26-59	43-168
PASSING YARDS (NET)	181	306
PASSES ATT-COMP-INT	34-15-1	35-18-1
TOTAL OFFENSE PLAYS-YARDS	60-240	78-474
PUNT RETURNS-YARDS	0-0	5-82
KICKOFF RETURNS-YARDS	6-98	2-72
PUNTS (NUMBER-AVG)	10-36.8	4-39.5
FUMBLES-LOST	1-1	2-0
PENALTIES-YARDS	10-52	7-48
POSSESSION TIME	24:45	35:15
SACKS BY (NUMBER-YARDS)	0-0	2-15

INDIVIDUAL OFFENSIVE STATISTICS

RUSHING: **LSU** — Joseph Addai 15-81; J. Justin Vincent 8-40; Michael Clayton 1-17; Shyrone Carey 3-11; Alley Broussard 7-11; Matt Mauck 7-10; Devery Henderson 1 minus-1; Marcus Randall 1 minus-1. **UL-Monroe** — Kevin Payne 16-64.

PASSING: **LSU** — Matt Mauck 13-28-1-153; Marcus Randall 5-7-0-153. **UL-Monroe** — Steven Jyles 14-30-1-180; Daniel DaPrato 1-4-0-1.

RECEIVING: **LSU** — Michael Clayton 6-152; Devery Henderson 4-32; Dwayne Bowe 2-39; Joseph Addai 2-21; Skyler Green 2-14; Donnie Jones 1-33; Demetri Robinson 1-15. **UL-Monroe** — Kevin Payne 5-40.

INDIVIDUAL DEFENSIVE STATISTICS

INTERCEPTIONS: **LSU** — Jack Hunt 1-31. **UL-Monroe** — Chris Harris 1-0.

SACKS (unassisted, assisted): **LSU** — LaRon Landry 1-0; Eric Alexander 1-0. **UL-Monroe** — none.

TACKLES (unassisted, assisted): **LSU** — Jack Hunt 4-5; Lionel Turner 5-3. **UL-Monroe** — Maurice Sonnier 7-5; John Winchester 8-3.

LSU
59

ARIZONA
13

RAZING ARIZONA

THE TIGERS OUTCLASS THEIR PAC-10 FOE IN A ONE-SIDED TRACK MEET

The Tigers take to the road for the first time this season, but the Wildcats hardly put up a fight. Cornerback Ronnie Prude, intercepting a pass, and the Tigers' defense actually was overshadowed by the performance of LSU's offense.

LSU 59
ARIZONA 13

LSU FANS WHO MADE THE TRIP NOT DISAPPOINTED

BY MIKE TRIPLETT STAFF WRITER

This was not the University of Arizona at Monroe. It only felt that way.

LSU supposedly was stepping up the competition in Week 2 of the 2003 season, but the Tigers' trip to Arizona quickly turned into the kind of rout they were expecting a week earlier against Louisiana-Monroe.

LSU cruised to a 59-13 victory in its first game against a Pac-10 opponent since 1984.

"I thought this would be a tough game for us," LSU coach Nick Saban said. "Arizona looked good and dominant last week (in a win over the University of Texas-El Paso). I expected them to move the ball on us a little and defensively give us some trouble.

"But when you get ahead early like we did, it changes the psychological disposition of a game."

There also was plenty of Tiger pride swarming the streets of Tucson, as thousands of LSU fans made the 1,300-mile trip to see the game. If the Tigers were rusty in that season opener, they were downright sparkling against the Wildcats, dominating in every phase of the game.

LSU scored on its first six offensive possessions, and at times the Tigers definitely were hitting on all cylinders:
▶ There were two long touchdown passes in the second quarter, a 48-yarder from Matt Mauck to Michael Clayton and a 55-yarder from Marcus Randall to Devery Henderson.
▶ There was a 62-yard punt-return touchdown by Skyler Green in the fourth quarter.
▶ There was a 47-yard field goal by redshirt freshman Ryan Gaudet in the first quarter.

At one point in the second quarter, LSU had outgained Arizona in yardage 306-34. By the end of the third quarter, LSU had 25 first downs and Arizona four.

LSU punted twice, both in the fourth quarter.

And everybody got into the mix.

Five tailbacks played, including Joseph Addai, who ran 18 times for 86 yards and two touchdowns. Backup Shyrone Carey rushed 10 times for 49 yards and a score. Justin Vincent, who at this point in the season was the third-string tailback, gained 44 total yards and rushed for a touchdown.

Mauck completed 10 of 11 passes for 150 yards. He threw for one touchdown and ran for another before calling it a day.

"I was pleased with the way Matt threw the ball and we ran the ball, and we had balance," Saban said. Randall, who entered with LSU leading 31-0, completed nine of 14 passes for 149 yards with a touchdown and an interception.

Clayton caught six passes for 109 yards and a touchdown. He even spent some of the night playing defense for the second time in his LSU career, lining up at safety when the Tigers switched to their nickel defense.

His second-quarter touchdown was his highlight. Mauck threw a 15-yard pass, and Clayton ran the final 40 yards or so into the end zone behind a pair of blockers.

Clayton made two similar plays against the Indians a week earlier at Tiger Stadium. The junior receiver again gave fans every indication that this was going to be a very special season.

AP TOP 10	
RANK, SCHOOL	**LAST WEEK**
1. OKLAHOMA	1
2. MIAMI (FLA.)	3
3. OHIO STATE	2
4. SOUTHERN CAL	4
5. MICHIGAN	5
6. TEXAS	6
7. KANSAS STATE	7
8. GEORGIA	8
9. VIRGINIA TECH	9
10. FLORIDA STATE	11
12. LSU	13

Released Sept. 7

AP PHOTO

Cornerback Ronnie Prude sacks Arizona's Nic Costa in the first quarter. LSU's defense put pressure on Arizona early and often, and the strategy paid off. The Wildcats weren't able to sustain anything on offense until late in the game when most starters were on the sidelines.

LSU	17	21	7	14	59
ARIZONA	0	0	0	13	13

SCORING SUMMARY

LSU Joseph Addai 1-yard run (Ryan Gaudet kick). Fifteen plays, 80 yards in 6:25

LSU Gaudet 47-yard field goal. Four plays, zero yards in 2:11

LSU Addai 8-yard run (Gaudet kick). Two plays, nine yards in 0:39

LSU Matt Mauck 4-yard run (Gaudet kick). Nine plays, 57 yards in 3:46

LSU Michael Clayton 48-yard pass from Mauck (Gaudet kick). Five plays, 80 yards in 2:11

LSU Devery Henderson 55-yard pass from Marcus Randall (Gaudet kick). Six plays, 80 yards in 2:24

LSU Shyrone Carey 1-yard run (Chris Jackson kick). Five plays, 38 yards in 1:57

LSU Justin Vincent 1-yard run (Jackson kick). Nine plays, 65 yards in 2:49

ARIZONA Zeonte Sherman 1-yard fumble recovery (Bobby Gill kick)

LSU Skyler Green 62-yard punt return (Jackson kick)

ARIZONA Clarence Farmer 11-yard run (Gill kick failed)

TEAM STATISTICS

CATEGORY	ARIZONA	LSU
FIRST DOWNS	10	28
RUSHES-YARDS (NET)	27-91	56-182
PASSING YARDS (NET)	91	299
PASSES ATT-COMP-INT	32-10-2	25-19-1
TOTAL OFFENSIVE PLAYS-YARDS	59-182	81-481
PUNT RETURNS-YARDS	2-4	7-120
KICKOFF RETURNS-YARDS	4-79	2-41
PUNTS (NUMBER-AVG)	10-40.0	2-47.0
FUMBLES-LOST	4-1	4-3
PENALTIES-YARDS	11-91	7-60
POSSESSION TIME	23:47	36:13
SACKS BY (NUMBER-YARDS)	3-26	2-14

INDIVIDUAL OFFENSIVE STATISTICS

RUSHING: **LSU** — Joseph Addai 18-86; Shyrone Carey 10-49; Barrington Edwards 9-34; Justin Vincent 6-18. **Arizona** — Clarence Farmer 8-61

PASSING: **LSU** — Marcus Randall 9-14-1-149; Matt Mauck 10-11-0-150 **Arizona** — Ryan O'Hara 7-20-1-70; Nic Costa 3-11-0-21; James Molina 0-1-1-0

RECEIVING: **LSU** — Michael Clayton 6-109; Devery Henderson 3-75; Dwayne Bowe 3-32; Skyler Green 2-28; Justin Vincent 2-26. **Arizona** — Sean Jones 3-27

INDIVIDUAL DEFENSIVE STATISTICS

INTERCEPTIONS: **LSU** — Travis Daniels 1-0; Ronnie Prude 1-0. **Arizona:** Darrell Brooks 1-0.

SACKS (unassisted-assisted): **LSU** — Marcus Spears 1-0; Lionel Turner 1-0. **Arizona** — Lamon Means 1-0; Andre Torrey 1-0.

SABAN LEAVES NO STONE UNTURNED IN PREPARATION

BY MIKE TRIPLETT STAFF WRITER

LSU cornerback Travis Daniels said he has often wondered when his coach sleeps.

He has seen Nick Saban's car parked outside of Tiger Stadium late at night. More important, he has seen the game plans the Tigers' defensive staff puts together every week.

"I know on Mondays or Tuesdays, we put in a bundle of stuff, then they start weeding out what they like, what they don't like or what we need to make adjustments to," Daniels said. "I don't think he goes to sleep. I think he does that stuff all night."

Saban said that's not the case. He said he doesn't function well if he doesn't get enough sleep. So he goes home when he gets tired around 10 or 11 p.m.

Then he starts fresh the next morning.

"I'm not the grinder that everybody makes me out to be," Saban said. "It might be grinding to you, to work from seven in the morning to 10 o'clock at night, a lot of days in a row. But that's coaching."

LSU coach Nick Saban enjoys the fruits of his labor, thanking Tigers fans after wrapping up the SEC West title with a 55–24 victory against Arkansas on Nov. 28 at Tiger Stadium.

STAFF PHOTO BY G. ANDREW BOYD

COACH NICK SABAN

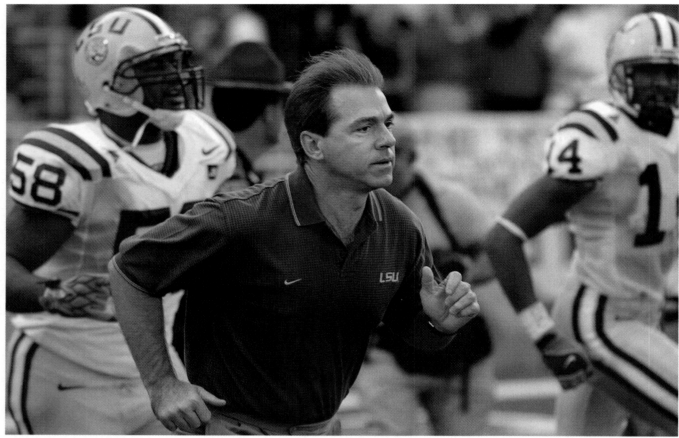

STAFF PHOTO BY ALEX BRANDON

When LSU takes the field, it's almost a sure bet coach Nick Saban has the Tigers prepared for anything.

The public sees the 52-year-old coach as a stern commander who is steering the program in the right direction. But not everybody gets to see his mind at work, during those long nights hunkered down in his office with defensive coordinator Will Muschamp and the rest of the Tigers' defensive staff.

"I think he's outstanding. One of the best I've ever worked with," said New England Patriots coach Bill Belichick, under whom Saban served as defensive coordinator for the Cleveland Browns from 1991-94. "I can tell you, I learned a lot from watching him coach and working with him. He's smart. He's got a great mind. He pays a lot of attention to detail.

"He's the kind of guy who's going to have every single base covered, every moving part. Some guys are good secondary coaches, some guys are good with the defensive line. But he understands what the corner is doing, what the out-

side linebacker is doing and how it all ties together. When you move one guy, he understands how it affects everybody else's reads and keys."

Saban played defensive back at Kent State before spending 21 years as a defensive coach in college and the NFL. He said he developed his philosophy from many of his mentors, including Belichick, George Perles, Earle Bruce and Don James.

The most apparent, though, is Belichick, one of the top defensive schemers in the NFL.

Saban said the main thing he learned from Belichick is "sleep deprivation." But he also learned his organizational structure. Saban sets aside specific blocks of time every week for things such as first-and-10 defense and second-and-long defense.

Saban said he spends about 80 percent of his time on defense.

"I try to contribute where I feel my experience and strength is, which has basically been defense and special teams," Saban said. "That's where I devote quite a bit of my time, trying to help in the planning and developing, and teaching it. The ultimate goal is to get the players to understand it."

The Tigers run an NFL-style defense. It's complex and sophisticated. Saban said that's necessary because college offenses have become as complex and sophisticated as NFL offenses.

The Tigers' defense relies on disguising coverages and blitzes — many, many blitzes.

"Coach is one of the best at it, man," LSU defensive end Marcus Spears said. "Sometimes you get in the game and things you've seen in practice is exactly how it happens in the game. I think that's the mark of great preparation. And all our coaches on the staff, those guys work every day, seven days a week, all day long.

"I'm pretty sure that when we get out there we know what we're doing."

Many LSU fans feel that their Tigers didn't get enough national respect this past year. But at least one national football writer — ESPN's Ivan Maisel — said he wouldn't count out Saban's defensive mind against anybody.

"Giving coach Nick Saban a month to develop a plan to stop any offense is worth seeing," Maisel wrote.

Daniels said Saban does more than just script a defense, though. Daniels said Saban is a terrific teacher, though he isn't always gentle and kind.

Saban chewed out Daniels after the defensive back let a man get open on the final play at Mississippi State this year — a game LSU won 41-6.

"He never stops coaching," Daniels said. "He preaches for us to play for 60 minutes, and I guess in return he's going to coach us for 60 minutes.

"Everything that I know right now, I kind of learned from coach Saban. In high school they're decent coaches, but they never taught you the technique and the fundamentals like coach Saban does. He breaks it all the way down."

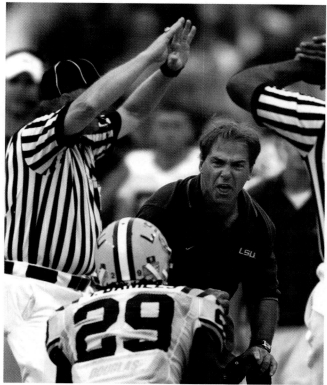

STAFF PHOTOS BY JOHN McCUSKER (TOP); ALEX BRANDON (ABOVE)

Top, coach Nick Saban says he spends about 80 percent of his time working on defense, his area of expertise. Above, Saban lets cornerback Travis Daniels know what he thinks of an in-game lapse — even though the Tigers had built a healthy lead.

LSU
35

WESTERN ILLINOIS
7

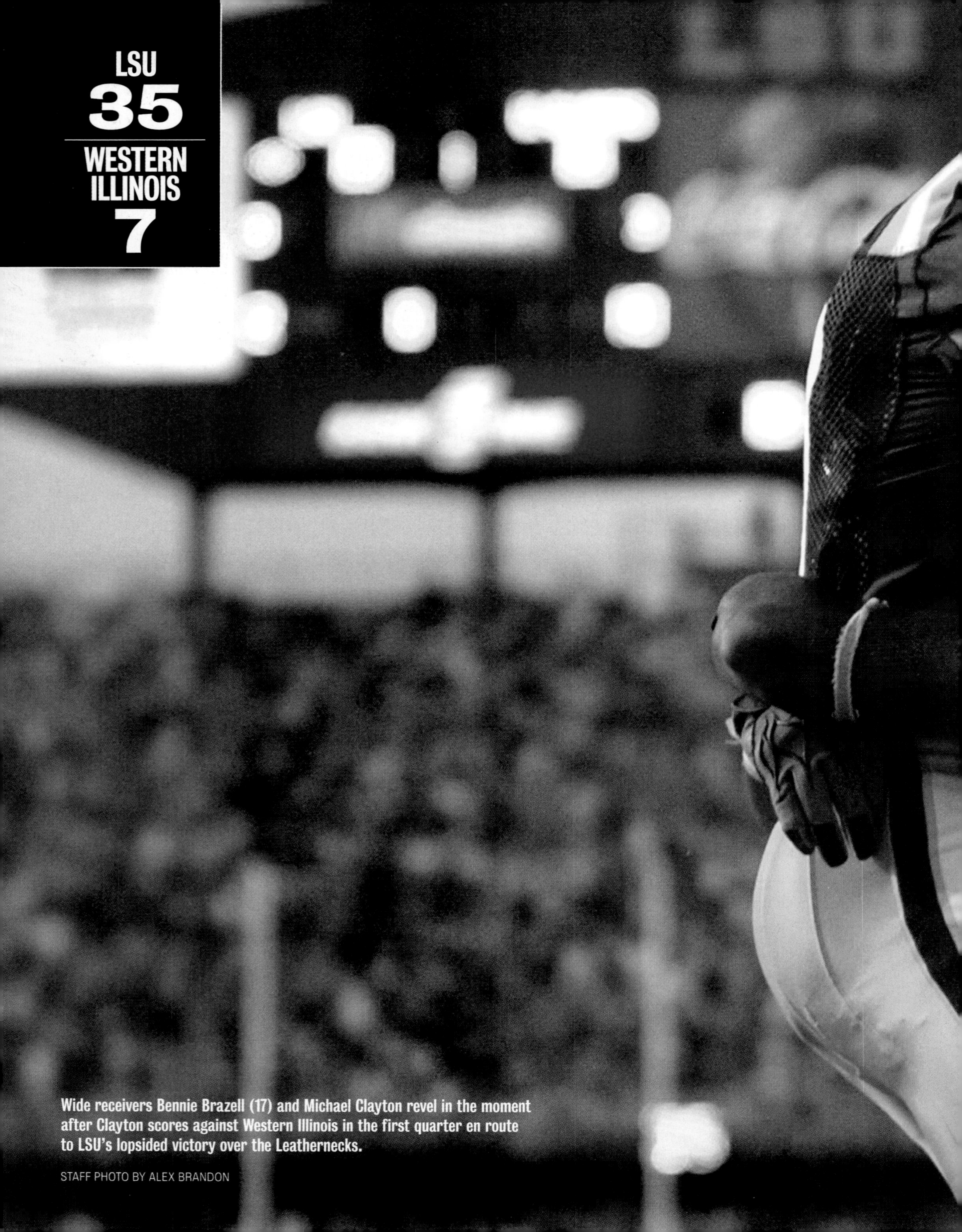

Wide receivers Bennie Brazell (17) and Michael Clayton revel in the moment after Clayton scores against Western Illinois in the first quarter en route to LSU's lopsided victory over the Leathernecks.

STAFF PHOTO BY ALEX BRANDON

THE TIGERS HANDLE
A DIVISION 1-AA FOE,
BUT IT WASN'T PRETTY

ROOM FOR IMPROVEMENT

LSU 35
W. ILLINOIS 7

LSU GETS REALITY CHECK JUST BEFORE CONFERENCE PLAY

BY MIKE TRIPLETT STAFF WRITER

LSU survived its final nonconference tune-up against Western Illinois, but only because the Tigers made their share of really good plays alongside some really bad ones.

But the performance turned in by the Tigers against the Division I-AA Leathernecks wouldn't be worth much in an SEC game. The 35-7 victory was a far cry from LSU's efficient dismantling of Arizona a week earlier.

Fumbles, penalties, missed field-goal attempts, a missed extra-point attempt, a botched snap, dropped passes, blown pass routes — you name it, the Tigers did it.

And coach Nick Saban let them know about it.

"I was very surprised with the way we played," said LSU receiver Michael Clayton, who still managed to continue his incredible run through LSU's nonconference schedule.

The junior receiver caught 11 passes for a career-high 162 yards and a touchdown — despite leaving with what he called a "tweaked" ankle in the third quarter.

"The mistakes we made were our fault," said Clayton, who dropped two passes. "It was nothing our opponents forced us to do. The (LSU) defense did a great job taking care of us."

Sophomore tailback Joseph Addai had the hardest day at the office. He fumbled twice in the first quarter when LSU was in scoring position — once at the Western Illinois 1-yard

Led by safety Jack Hunt (8), the Tigers swarm to the ball, leaving the Leathernecks feeling closed in as LSU's defense continued to shine.

STAFF PHOTO BY ALEX BRANDON

line. After the second fumble, he was sent to the bench for the next two quarters. Meanwhile his replacement, Shyrone Carey, filled in nicely with 124 yards and a touchdown on 21 carries.

But there were other miscues. Receiver Devery Henderson added a fumble in the third quarter.

Redshirt freshman kicker Ryan Gaudet took a seat on the bench after he had an extra-point attempt blocked and missed a 45-yard field-goal attempt wide left.

He was replaced by freshman Chris Jackson, who missed a 34-yard field-goal attempt wide left.

LSU long-snapper Steve Damen snapped the ball over punter Donnie Jones' head. The Tigers allowed Western Illinois to recover an onside kick to open the second half. The Leathernecks scored a touchdown on that drive, bringing the score within too-close-for-comfort range at 13-7.

AP TOP 10	
RANK, SCHOOL	**LAST WEEK**
1. OKLAHOMA	1
2. MIAMI (FLA.)	2
3. MICHIGAN	5
4. SOUTHERN CAL	4
5. OHIO STATE	3
6. KANSAS STATE	7
7. GEORGIA	8
8. VIRGINIA TECH	9
9. PITTSBURGH	11
10. FLORIDA STATE	10
11. LSU	12

Released Sept. 14

"We obviously made some mistakes that were critical in the game, fumbling twice in the red area in the first half, missing two field goals, having a bad snap on a PAT, having a bad snap on a punt, not having very good kickoff coverage, letting them get an onside kick," Saban said. "I mean, this is as poorly as we played on special teams, I think, for a long time.

"But they're all things that we can correct. They're all things that we can correct on offense, too."

Junior quarterback Matt Mauck completed 23 passes for 305 yards and a career-high four touchdown passes. He also ran in a two-point conversion.

Once the Tigers finally shook off their offensive mishaps, the offense was efficient in the third and fourth quarters. After Henderson's fumble, the Tigers scored touchdowns on three consecutive drives.

"I think Matt Mauck probably played as fine a game as I've seen him play since he's been our quarterback," Saban

said. "He made some outstanding reads today and some very good throws when things weren't going so well out there.

"And Shyrone Carey had as good a day as he's had since he's been a player here. And Michael Clayton had over 150 yards in pass receiving.

"We need to be a little more consistent, and we need to eliminate some of the bad plays. All the things that happened can be corrected. And we'll get to work on trying to do that."

LSU's defense was terrific at times, holding Western Illinois' offense to 208 yards and 12 first downs. Cornerback

STAFF PHOTO BY ALEX BRANDON

Despite Western Illinois' best efforts, LSU running back Shyrone Carey finds the corner and plenty of room against the Leathernecks. Carey finished with 124 yards on 21 carries.

Corey Webster intercepted two passes, and freshman safety LaRon Landry intercepted a third pass in the end zone in the fourth quarter.

Even the special teams made a positive impact. The Tigers blocked a punt in the first quarter for the first time since 1999. And they blocked a field-goal attempt in the second quarter for the first time since '98.

WESTERN ILL.	0	0	7	0	7
LSU	6	7	15	7	35

SCORING SUMMARY

LSU Michael Clayton 10-yard pass from Matt Mauck (Ryan Gaudet kick failed). Ten plays, 58 yards in 4:49

LSU Shyrone Carey 1-yard run (Chris Jackson kick). Eight plays, 53 yards in 2:26

WESTERN ILLINOIS Terrence Hall 3-yard pass from Russ Michna (Justin Langan kick). Nine plays, 47 yards in 4:51

LSU Skyler Green 8-yard pass from Mauck (Mauck rush). Eight plays, 59 yards in 3:52

LSU Green 40-yard pass from Mauck (Jackson kick). One play, 40 yards in 8 seconds

LSU Devery Henderson 16-yard pass from Mauck (Jackson kick). Thirteen plays, 62 yards in 5:27

TEAM STATISTICS

CATEGORY	WESTERN ILL.	LSU
FIRST DOWNS	12	31
RUSHES-YARDS (NET)	25-13	43-152
PASSING YARDS (NET)	195	305
PASSES ATT-COMP-INT	39-17-3	32-23-0
TOTAL OFFENSIVE PLAYS-YARDS	64-208	75-457
FUMBLE RETURNS-YARDS	1-29	0-0
PUNT RETURNS-YARDS	0-0	4-37
KICKOFF RETURNS-YARDS	4-80	1-33
PUNTS (NUMBER-AVG)	6-28.5	0-0.0
FUMBLES-LOST	0-0	5-3
PENALTIES-YARDS	12-75	3-35
POSSESSION TIME	27:59	32:01
SACKS BY (NUMBER-YARDS)	2-2	2-14

INDIVIDUAL OFFENSIVE STATISTICS

RUSHING: **LSU** — Shyrone Carey 21-124; Joseph Addai 8-29; Devery Henderson 1-13; Justin Vincent 6-6; Marcus Randall 1-5; Matt Mauck 5-2; team 1 minus-27. **Western Ill.** — Travis Glasford 16-21.

PASSING: **LSU** — Matt Mauck 23-32-0-305. **Western Ill.** — Russ Michna 17-39-3-195

RECEIVING: **LSU** — Michael Clayton 11-162; Devery Henderson 6-65; Skyler Green 3-54; Shyrone Carey 1-10; Craig Davis 1-9; Eric Edwards 1-5. **Western Ill.** — Terrence Hall 5-36; Travis Glasford 4-43

INDIVIDUAL DEFENSIVE STATISTICS

INTERCEPTIONS: **LSU** — Corey Webster 2-13; LaRon Landry 1-0. **Western Ill.** — none

SACKS (unassisted-assisted): **LSU** — Eric Alexander 1-0; Chad Lavalais 1-0. **Western Ill.** — Mike O'Brien 1-0

TACKLES (unassisted-assisted): **LSU** — Lionel Turner 3-4; Chad Lavalais 3-4; Travis Daniels 2-7; Ronnie Prude 2-4; Corey Webster 3-1; Cameron Vaughn 2-3; Chris Jackson 2-0; Brian West 2-0; Eric Alexander 2-1; Marcus Spears 1-1. **Western Ill.** — Lee Russell 6-6; Travis Washington 5-6; Drew Kocsis 4-4; Chris McNutt 3-6; Phil Archer 2-8; Shamon Jamerson 5-1

29

HAPPY ENDING

TIGERS COME UP WITH BIG PLAYS LATE IN CONFERENCE OPENER

With early supremacy in the Southeastern Conference at stake, receiver Skyler Green hauls in a 34-yard touchdown pass to give LSU the upper hand against Georgia with 1:22 remaining. On the play, Green improvised after running the wrong route.

STAFF PHOTO BY ALEX BRANDON

LSU
17

GEORGIA
10

LSU	17
GEORGIA	10

LATE TOUCHDOWN, INTERCEPTION HELP SAVE THE DAY

BY MIKE TRIPLETT STAFF WRITER

LSU's winning touchdown was a mistake. It was never supposed to happen. And really, could there have been a more fitting finale to this game?

The Tigers' 17-10 victory over defending Southeastern Conference champion Georgia was a redemption song. It was filled with second chances for both teams.

But none was a better case of poetic justice than Matt Mauck's 34-yard touchdown pass to Skyler Green with 1:22 remaining before a Tiger Stadium crowd of 92,251.

Green, a sophomore receiver, had dropped three passes earlier in the game. Mauck, a junior quarterback, had just fumbled away a chance to ice the game on LSU's previous drive.

And Georgia had just tied the score at 10 with a 93-yard screen pass against an LSU defense that had been dominant all afternoon.

But then Green ran the wrong route, and everything was right in Death Valley.

"It was actually supposed to be a pick play, where Skyler picks (Michael Clayton's defender)," explained Mauck, who said Green was "option zero" on the play. "I don't know if Skyler heard the wrong play or if he was running something different. But he just ran right by the guy. And I barely saw

With less than one minute remaining, cornerback Corey Webster (13) intercepted a pass from Georgia's David Greene at LSU's 22-yard line. With the outcome no longer in doubt, the Tigers rejoice.

STAFF PHOTO BY ALEX BRANDON

him out of the corner of my eye, threw it up there, and he made a great play."

The play came on third-and-four from the Georgia 34-yard line. LSU coach Nick Saban said he had not yet decided if he would attempt a 51-yard field goal on fourth down.

He didn't have to.

Green admitted that he confused the called play with a similar play. He ran a flag route, realized his mistake midway through the play and decided to keep running.

"I just kept going full-speed, just kept the play going and just stepped up and made the play," said Green, who caught two touchdown passes the previous week against Western Illinois and returned a punt for a touchdown at Arizona the week before. "When I saw Matt release, I told myself, 'I can't drop this one.' That's all I told myself, 'I'm not going to drop this one.' "

Green caught the ball, but LSU still had not sealed the game until

STAFF PHOTO BY ALEX BRANDON

LSU safety Jack Hunt (8) and defensive end Bryce Wyatt show Georgia's Tyson Browning who's in charge. The Bulldogs were able to gain only 97 yards on 31 carries against the Tigers.

cornerback Corey Webster intercepted a pass by Georgia quarterback David Greene at the LSU 22-yard line with less than a minute remaining.

The Bulldogs must have had a long trip home, thinking of the missed opportunities in Baton Rouge.

With LSU's offense floundering from the start, Georgia entered the Tigers' territory five times in the first half and came away with just three points.

One time LSU defensive end Marcus Spears caused a Greene fumble at the LSU 8-yard line. Three other times, Georgia kicker Billy Bennett missed field-goal attempts.

"We had a great chance today," said receiver Reggie Brown, whose Bulldogs entered the game ranked No. 7. "But

we never capitalized on the opportunities we had. Dropped balls, everything. Too many mistakes. You know when you should have scored, and we had a bunch."

LSU's offense was equally inept in the first half, failing to get past Georgia's 46-yard line until the final five minutes of the half. Mauck threw an interception in the first quarter, and the Tigers punted six times before the break.

But in those final five minutes of the half, LSU finally put together a drive. Mauck hit Green with a 31-yard pass on third-and-nine. And junior tailback Shyrone Carey followed with a 9-yard carry and a 21-yard touchdown run, giving LSU a 7-3 lead at halftime.

"I don't know if we were a little anxious in the beginning

of the game, but we were a little out of sorts at the start," Saban said. "To compete the way we did, to get ahead in the game, to overcome the adversity we had in the first half, to have them have a (93-yard) touchdown pass (after Mauck's fumble) and then to come right back and make the plays we needed to score a touchdown and get back ahead in the game — I'm certainly proud of the way we did that.

"I think if you're going to really beat good teams, you've got to be able to do that, because nobody just dominates a good team."

LSU's defense took command in the second half, throwing off Greene, Georgia's All-SEC quarterback, with relentless blitzes. The Tigers batted down seven passes at the line of scrimmage and intercepted two passes.

When Greene was sidelined for two series with a knee injury, LSU sacked his backup, D.J. Shockley, twice and pressured him into an intentional-grounding penalty.

But Georgia's defense was equally persistent, and the Tigers had to settle for one field goal — a 47-yarder by Ryan Gaudet that was good by about a foot — and one blocked field-goal attempt.

Finally, LSU was in scoring position late in the fourth quarter with a 10-3 lead, but Mauck fumbled after running for a first down to the Georgia 15-yard line.

Two plays later, Greene hit Tyson Browning with a screen pass, and Browning used key blocks to run 93 yards for the touchdown.

LSU responded with a 48-yard kickoff return by Devery Henderson, setting up the redemption pass from Mauck to Green.

"I felt horrible watching that guy run down the sideline, scoring a touchdown after I had fumbled," Mauck said. "I just really wanted an opportunity to help the team out after such a crucial turnover.

"We made up for some of the mistakes we made earlier in the game."

AP TOP 10

RANK, SCHOOL	LAST WEEK
1. OKLAHOMA	1
2. MIAMI (FLA.)	2
3. SOUTHERN CAL	4
4. OHIO STATE	5
5. VIRGINIA TECH	8
6. FLORIDA STATE	10
7. LSU	11
8. TENNESSEE	12
9. ARKANSAS	14
10. OREGON	22

Released Sept. 21

	1	2	3	4	
GEORGIA	3	0	0	7	10
LSU	0	7	3	7	17

SCORING SUMMARY

GEORGIA Billy Bennett 33-yard field goal. Seven plays, 36 yards in 1:25

LSU Shyrone Carey 21-yard run (Ryan Gaudet kick). Six plays, 85 in 2:08

LSU Gaudet 47-yard field goal. Ten plays, 51 yards in 5:29

GEORGIA Tyson Browning 93-yard pass from David Greene (Billy Bennett kick). One play, 85 yards in 27 seconds

LSU Skyler Green 34-yard pass from Matt Mauck (Ryan Gaudet kick). Six plays, 51 yards in 2:54

TEAM STATISTICS

CATEGORY	GEORGIA	LSU
FIRST DOWNS	23	16
RUSHES-YARDS (NET)	31-97	43-105
PASSING YARDS (NET)	314	180
PASSES ATT-COMP-INT	46-20-2	29-14-1
TOTAL OFFENSIVE PLAYS-YARDS	77-411	72-285
FUMBLES-LOST	1-1	2-1
KICKOFF RETURNS-YARDS	2-34	3-86
PUNTS (NUMBER-AVG)	6-41.3	8-40.2
FUMBLES-LOST	1-1	2-1
PENALTIES-YARDS	7-48	9-63
POSSESSION TIME	26:43	33:17
SACKS BY (NUMBER-YARDS)	1-9	4-27

INDIVIDUAL OFFENSIVE STATISTICS

RUSHING: **LSU** — Shyrone Carey 18-73; Joseph Addai 15-65; D. Henderson 1 minus-1; Matt Mauck 5 minus-3. **Georgia** — Michael Cooper 18-73; Tyson Browning 3-20

PASSING: **LSU** — Matt Mauck 14-29-1-180. **Georgia** — David Greene 20-44-2-314; D.J. Shockley 0-2-0-0

RECEIVING: **LSU** — Skyler Green 4-78; Eric Edwards 3-41; Michael Clayton 2-23; Devery Henderson 2-16; Joseph Addai 2-9. **Georgia** — Damien Gary 7-80; Reggie Brown 7-78; Tyson Browning 2-104

INDIVIDUAL DEFENSIVE STATISTICS

INTERCEPTIONS: **LSU** — Corey Webster 1-10; Lionel Turner 1-3. **Georgia** — Sean Jones 1-0

SACKS (unassisted-assisted): **LSU** — Cameron Vaughn 1-0; Marquise Hill 1-0; Chad Lavalais 1-0; Kirston Pittman 1-0. **Georgia** — Quentin Moses 1-0; David Pollack 0-1

TACKLES (unassisted-assisted): **LSU** — Jack Hunt 6-4; Corey Webster 7-2; Travis Daniels 5-2; Eric Alexander 5-1; Lionel Turner 4-2; Cameron Vaughn 4-1; Bryce Wyatt 4-1; Chad Lavalais 3-2. **Georgia** — Sean Jones 10-2; Thomas Davis 8-2; Bruce Thornton 5-3; Odell Thurman 6-1

It took awhile, but quarterback Matt Mauck (18) and LSU's offense got the upper hand against Georgia. Mauck, who completed 14 of 29 passes, was able to find that winning touch in the fourth quarter.

STAFF PHOTO BY ALEX BRANDON

TIGERS, MAUCK DON'T CRACK WHEN GOING GETS TOUGH

BY PETER FINNEY
COLUMNIST

Matthew Ryan Mauck, the winning quarterback, looked down, searching for the right words, then put it all in one simple declarative sentence.

"This was a next-play game," he said.

And so it was, a 17-10 victory that began, from the standpoint of the 92,251 folks sitting in Tiger Stadium, as a study in boredom and wound up as a fingernail-biting classic right out of the textbook of Nick "One Play at a Time" Saban.

One moment, Mauck was fumbling away a chance to add to a 10-3 lead that would have put the Georgia Bulldogs away with four minutes to go.

The next, Mauck stayed cool in the face of a rush long enough to find Skyler Green for 34 yards and the winning points in the final 82 seconds.

In between, the Bulldogs, with unexpected suddenness, had silenced the home crowd with an other-worldly 93-yard touchdown, a pass David Greene fired from out of his end zone into the arms of Tyson Browning, who caught the ball at the 10 and ran past the Georgia bench to make it a 10-10 game.

"When I came off the field after that fumble," Mauck said, "Coach looked at me and said, 'Forget it. Next time, we score.' With Coach, it's always next play."

Sounds simple. But look. Saturday it's 10-10 and then came "the next play."

STAFF PHOTO BY ALEX BRANDON

Despite the fact that wide receiver Skyler Green had dropped a couple of passes earlier against Georgia, quarterback Matt Mauck (18) still had confidence in him. After the Bulldogs tied the score at 10, Mauck scrambled to his left and connected with Green for a touchdown that provided the winning points.

STAFF PHOTO BY ALEX BRANDON

Determined to reach the goal line, running back Shyrone Carey scores on a 21-yard run in the second quarter to give the Tigers the lead. Carey finished with 73 yards on 18 carries.

Devery Henderson takes the kickoff at the goal line and returns it to midfield.

"That was a tremendous momentum shift," said Georgia's Thomas Davis. "It made it so much easier for them and brought the crowd back in the game."

Suddenly, Shyrone Carey is dancing to the outside, and the Tigers are moving, as is the clock, with the Tigers facing a third-and-four at the Georgia 34.

So what exactly did Mauck say the "next play" should be called?

He laughed. "How about: 'What's he doing?' Yes."

That's pretty much what happened. Mauck's primary receiver was Michael Clayton, who was supposed to run a curl over the middle. On the play, Green was supposed to function as a "pick" to free Clayton. But there went Green, running across the middle, using his speed to pull away from a red jersey, and there went Mauck, with the presence of mind to find his 5-foot-10 target in the end zone.

"It could not have happened to a better guy," Mauck said. "Skyler had a few drops early, and he felt just as bad as I did when I coughed it up. I fumble, and the guys are patting me on the back. It was the same with Skyler. He used his skills and his instincts to come up with a big play at the right time. It's just like Coach Saban says: 'Whatever happens, you play the next play, and you do it for 60 minutes.'"

Ask Corey Webster — the Tiger who sewed up Saturday's victory with a Hall of Fame interception when quarterback Greene had the Bulldogs on the move.

STAFF PHOTO BY ALEX BRANDON

LSU running back Joseph Addai, who finished with 65 yards on 15 carries, takes off during the third quarter. With both defenses living up to their hype, rushing yards were scarce.

In 2002's final-minute loss to Arkansas, which kept LSU out of the SEC championship game, Webster's mental lapse allowed the Razorbacks a 50-yard completion that set up the winning score.

Not this time. This time, Webster was running down the sideline in one-on-one coverage against Reggie Brown. Greene delivered a strike, and for a moment, it looked like the Bulldogs would be in business around the Tigers' 20.

"I'm watching his eyes," Webster said. "And I'm using what Coach likes to call 'ball skills.' "

Whatever it was, Webster tipped the ball out of Brown's clutches, and took it away, all in one motion as he back-pedaled.

That was it.

After losing his first game in nine outings on the road, Georgia coach Mark Richt said, "Big games usually come down to big plays, and LSU made most of them. You've got to give them credit."

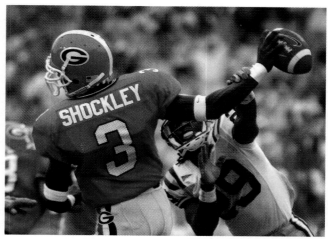

STAFF PHOTO BY ALEX BRANDON

Talk about a shock to the system. LSU defensive back Travis Daniels brings the heat against Georgia backup quarterback D.J. Shockley.

As it turned out, the Tigers were fortunate to go into half-time leading 7-3. Before LSU marched 85 yards for a second-quarter touchdown, the Tigers had managed two first downs and had 48 yards in total offense, including 2 yards rushing.

"The defense kept us in the game," Mauck said. "I don't know if I've ever seen so many passes deflected at the line as they came up with."

The biggest came early when Chad Lavalais batted away a Greene pass over the middle, one headed to a wide-open receiver who could have walked in for six points.

"We knew if we kept our hands up against a guy like Greene, we could do some damage," Lavalais said. "He's hard to get to, and he gets rid of the ball in a hurry. Against a guy like him, you always have to be thinking hands-up more than thinking sack."

In a way, for the Tigers it was hands-up and heads-up against an outstanding football team that, who knows, could be waiting in Atlanta in December for an encore in the SEC title game.

Of course, don't suggest such a turn of events to Nick Saban.

Not now.

Right now, the LSU coach will tell you Mississippi State, waiting next week in Starkville, is as good as it gets in a next-play season.

#18 MATT MAUCK

Matt Mauck has seen LSU football from all angles. As a freshman in 2001, he came off the bench to lead the Tigers to an upset of No. 2 Tennessee in the SEC championship game in Atlanta. As a sophomore starter last season, Mauck had the Tigers rolling to an impressive win at Florida before an injury cut his season short.

But in 2003, he put it all together with a superb season that helped carry the Tigers to the SEC championship and a victory against Oklahoma in the BCS championship game in the Sugar Bowl at the Superdome. Not bad for someone who's not even sure if he'll return for his senior season, possibly opting instead for dental school.

But for now, Mauck has helped lead the Tigers into the national spotlight.

"It's just such a great atmosphere to be a part of. It's such a great thing to go through with your team," said Mauck, who set a school record with 28 touchdown passes this season, including three games in which he matched the school record of four.

After directing a second SEC championship game victory in three years, Mauck said, "All we could do is play the best game we could play against Georgia, and hopefully somebody will take notice."

Don't worry, they have, especially LSU's fans.

"I think they deserve it," Mauck said. "We've got great fans here who are passionate about football. They've been a great part of our success."

Now the question remains: Will Mauck decide to drill receivers downfield next year or teeth? — Mike Triplett

FULL NAME: Matthew Ryan Mauck
BORN: Feb. 12, 1979
BIRTHPLACE: Evansville, Ind.
ATTENDED: Jasper (Ind.) High School
FAMILY: Parents are Roger and Kathy Mauck. One brother, Geoff, and one sister, Libby
MAJOR: Pre-medicine
POSITION: Quarterback
HEIGHT: 6 feet 2
WEIGHT: 213 pounds

CAREER STATISTICS

YEAR	GAMES	STARTS	ATT.	COMP.	YARDS	TDS	INT.
2001	3	0	41	18	224	0	2
2002	6	6	130	63	782	9	2
2003	14	14	358	229	2,825	28	14

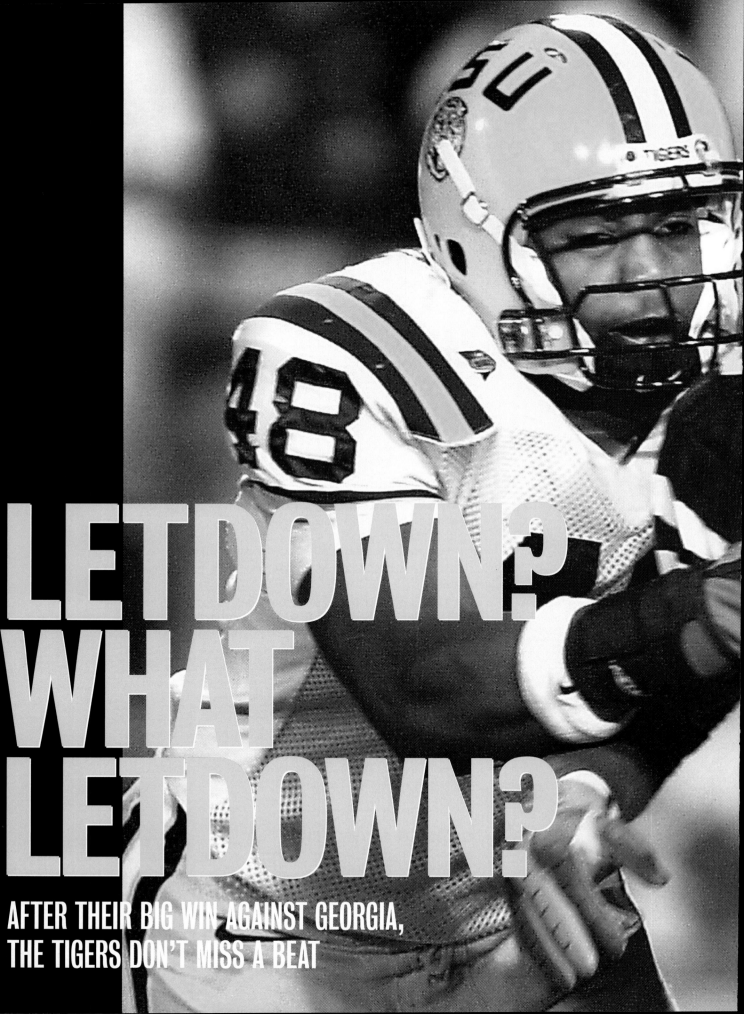

LETDOWN? WHAT LETDOWN?

AFTER THEIR BIG WIN AGAINST GEORGIA,
THE TIGERS DON'T MISS A BEAT

GAME 5 | SEPTEMBER 27, 2003

DAVIS WADE STADIUM | STARKVILLE, MISS.

Defensive end Jarvus Ryes, bringing down running back Fred Reid, and the Tigers grasp the concept: Stop the run. LSU's defense shined, holding the Bulldogs to 31 yards on 30 carries.

AP PHOTO

LSU
41

MISS. STATE
6

LSU 41
MISS. ST. 6

TIGERS CAPITALIZE ON OUTMANNED BULLDOGS' MISTAKES

BY MIKE TRIPLETT STAFF WRITER

After a big win against Georgia the previous week, LSU followed up with an even more impressive win over Mississippi State, jumping to a 34-point lead and pulling most of its starters by the third quarter.

While LSU coach Nick Saban had worried about a letdown after the Tigers' win over Georgia a week earlier, the Tigers turned in an even more thorough and efficient performance in hammering Mississippi State 41-6.

"Actually, we practiced better this week than we did the week of the Georgia game," Saban said. "I was pleased with the way we practiced. I was pleased with our attention to detail. I was pleased with the energy level we had in pregame warmups and went out and played with.

"This team has competed well."

Saban spoke all week about trying to develop a team that can give the same level of performance, no matter the opponent.

Whatever he's selling, the Tigers are buying.

Receiver Michael Clayton pointed out that the Tigers can play better than they did. And he pointed out that LSU was not satisfied with a 24-0 halftime lead.

Within six minutes of the third quarter, LSU had increased its lead to 34-0.

"We knew they weren't going to give up. It was a must for us to come out and dominate in the second half," said

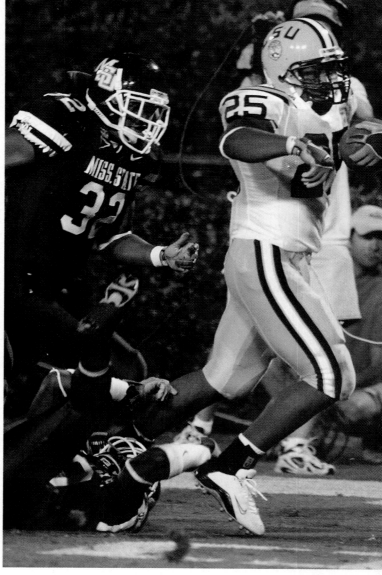

AP PHOTO

On a night when LSU's offense finds the going easy, Justin Vincent tops off the onslaught with a 3-yard touchdown run in the fourth quarter. Vincent led the Tigers in rushing with 58 yards on six carries.

Clayton, who caught three passes for 31 yards and drew more of his usual attention from the opposing defense.

As a result, receiver Devery Henderson had the biggest day on offense, catching a career-high seven passes for 114 yards and a touchdown.

"We've still got to work out some kinks," Clayton said. "There were times when we hurt ourselves."

Mostly, the Tigers spent the night putting a hurtin' on Mississippi State, which absorbed its ninth straight loss and would go on to finish the season 2-10.

LSU was both efficient and opportunistic, winning the turnover contest four to two. Whenever Mississippi State slipped up, LSU took advantage:

▶ When Mississippi State quarterback Kevin Fant overthrew his intended receiver in the second quarter, LSU safety Jack Hunt intercepted the pass and returned the ball 34 yards to the 1-yard line. Shyrone Carey followed with his second 1-yard touchdown run, giving LSU a 17-0 lead.

▶ Later in the second quarter, Fant's dump-off pass was tipped by receiver Justin Jenkins. This time LSU safety Travis Daniels intercepted the pass and returned the ball 48 yards for a score and a 24-0 lead.

▶ On the third play of the third quarter, Daniels recovered a fumble by Bulldogs receiver McKinley Scott. And on the next play, LSU quarterback Matt Mauck threw a 36-yard touchdown pass to Henderson for a 31-0 lead.

Following a 37-yard field goal by Ryan Gaudet — his second of the night — LSU led 34-0 and the starters called it an early night.

"Every team that has played LSU so far has had from 60-some-odd snaps to 77. But nobody's been able to sustain running the football," said Mississippi State coach Jackie Sherill, whose Bulldogs rushed for 31 yards on 30 carries. "When you get one-dimensional, you have big problems against them, because they're able to bring their blitzes."

LSU's defense continued its dominance, holding Mississippi State scoreless for three quarters. The Tigers sacked Fant four times in the third quarter.

LSU topped the victory with a touchdown run by freshman Justin Vincent. Vincent led the Tigers in rushing with 58 yards on six carries. Mauck completed 12 of 19 passes for 171 yards with one touchdown and one interception.

AP TOP 10

RANK, SCHOOL	LAST WEEK
1. OKLAHOMA	1
2. MIAMI (FLA.)	2
3. OHIO STATE	4
4. VIRGINIA TECH	5
5. FLORIDA STATE	6
6. LSU	7
7. TENNESSEE	8
8. ARKANSAS	9
9. MICHIGAN	11
10. SOUTHERN CAL	3

Released Sept. 28

LSU	7	17	10	7	41
MISS. STATE	0	0	0	6	6

SCORING SUMMARY

LSU Shyrone Carey 1-yard run (Ryan Gaudet kick). Eight plays, 65 yards in 3:24

LSU Gaudet 32-yard field goal. Nine plays, 43 yards in 2:55

LSU Carey 1-yard run (Gaudet kick). One play, 1 yard in 5 seconds

LSU Travis Daniels 48-yard interception return (Gaudet kick)

LSU Devery Henderson 36-yard pass from Matt Mauck (Gaudet kick). One play, 36 yards in 8 seconds

LSU Gaudet 37-yard field goal. Nine plays, 43 yards in 3:35

MISSISSIPPI STATE Justin Jenkins 15-yard pass from Kevin Fant (Fant pass failed). Ten plays, 92 yards in 4:30

LSU Justin Vincent 3-yard run (Gaudet kick). Eight plays, 68 yards in 4:13

TEAM STATISTICS

CATEGORY	MISS. STATE	LSU
FIRST DOWNS	18	17
RUSHES-YARDS (NET)	30-31	35-163
PASSING YARDS (NET)	208	191
PASSES ATT-COMP-INT	39-21-2	25-14-1
TOTAL OFFENSE PLAYS-YARDS	69-239	60-354
PUNT RETURNS-YARDS	3-13	5-41
KICKOFF RETURNS-YARDS	5-106	2-49
PUNTS (NUMBER-AVG)	7-40.7	5-44.0
FUMBLES-LOST	3-2	1-1
PENALTIES-YARDS	9-70	6-66
POSSESSION TIME	32:54	27:06
SACKS BY (NUMBER-YARDS)	1-9	5-41

INDIVIDUAL OFFENSIVE STATISTICS

RUSHING: **LSU** — Justin Vincent 6-58; Shyrone Carey 13-50; Joseph Addai 10-25; Skyler Green 1-15; Barrington Edwards 2-13; Matt Mauck 1-5; Marcus Randall 2 minus-3. **Miss. State** — Fred Reid 6-29; Nick Turner 10-23

PASSING: **LSU** — Matt Mauck 12-19-1-171; Marcus Randall 2-6-0-20. **Miss. State** — Kevin Fant 19-30-2-191; Kyle York 2-9-0-17

RECEIVING: **LSU** — Devery Henderson 7-114; Michael Clayton 3-31; Skyler Green 2-28; Dwayne Bowe 2-18. **Miss. State** — Ray Ray Bivines 6-53; Justin Jenkins 5-61

INDIVIDUAL DEFENSIVE STATISTICS

INTERCEPTIONS: **LSU** — Jack Hunt 1-34; Travis Daniels 1-48. **Miss. State** — Odell Bradley 1-14

SACKS (unassisted-assisted): **LSU** — Randall Gay 1-0; Chad Lavalais 1-0; Dave Peterson 0-1; Cameron Vaughn 0-1; Melvin Oliver 0-1; Travis Daniels 1-0; Kyle Williams 1-0. **Miss. State** — Tommy Kelly 0-1; Willie Evans 1-0

TACKLES (unassisted-assisted): **LSU** — LaRon Landry 8-3; Travis Daniels 6-0; Jack Hunt 5-1; Corey Webster 4-2; Lionel Turner 3-2; Chad Lavalais 3-1; Cameron Vaughn 3-1; Marcus Spears 2-2; Eric Alexander 3-0 **Miss. State** — Ronald Fields 6-2; T.J. Mawhinney 5-3; Jeramie Johnson 5-0; Marvin Byrdsong 4-1

FLORIDA
19

LSU
7

With expectations
running high,
the Tigers and
quarterback Matt Mauck
aren't able to rise
to the challenge
against the Gators.

GAME 6 | OCTOBER 11, 2003

TIGER STADIUM | BATON ROUGE

GATOR RAID

STRUGGLING FLORIDA INVADES TIGER STADIUM AND HANDS LSU ITS ONLY LOSS

FLORIDA	19
LSU	7

TIGERS CAN'T REGAIN WINNING FORM AFTER A WEEK OFF

BY MIKE TRIPLETT STAFF WRITER

When it finally rained, it poured. The dark clouds above Tiger Stadium threatened all afternoon until a shower finally dumped on LSU's fans and players as they exited the field — a fitting finale to LSU's 19-7 loss to Florida.

The Tigers had avoided disaster all season, coming into the game with a 5-0 record. But Saturday's loss was a total collapse, a complete team effort.

Receivers ran the wrong routes. The quarterback made poor throws. Defenders missed their assignments. The running game was non-existent. The Tigers had 13 penalties for 99 yards.

And just like that, the Tigers were reminded how difficult it is to maintain a perfect season.

"It's OK to make one mistake," LSU receiver Michael Clayton said. "They say it's OK to make one mistake, but if everybody makes one mistake, that's 11 mistakes, and that's kind of what we were dealing with today."

The Tigers' only touchdown came early in the first quarter when Skyler Green returned a punt 80 yards for a touchdown.

LSU's offense only crossed midfield four times, and three of those drives ended with turnovers. Matt Mauck threw two interceptions, and receiver Devery Henderson fumbled after a 41-yard reception.

And the turnovers weren't half as bad as the penalties.

In the third quarter, LSU had a 42-yard pass play that was

Despite LSU coach Nick Saban's preaching earlier in the week to stay focused, the Tigers' play is sloppy, leaving Saban and defensive coordinator Will Muschamp at a loss.

STAFF PHOTO
BY ALEX BRANDON

STAFF PHOTO BY ALEX BRANDON

LSU defensive tackle Chad Lavalais sacks Florida's Chris Leak during the third quarter, but the freshman quarterback stayed poised, finishing with 229 passing yards and two touchdowns.

called back on a holding penalty against guard Nate Livings. Then the defense allowed a Florida drive to continue because of a late hit by linebacker Lionel Turner.

"Obviously I'm very disappointed in the way we played in the game. I'm responsible for that," LSU coach Nick Saban said. "We didn't do a very good job of playing with the intensity we need. We didn't have any sense of urgency about what we were doing. We didn't play very smart in the game.

"We had 13 penalties, and I swear we probably had more than that. So it's very disappointing."

Saban said he felt like a "carnival preacher" trying to convince everyone from the LSU fans to his own players that they wouldn't be able to walk over Florida for an easy win.

The Gators came limping in with a 3-3 record and a freshman quarterback, Chris Leak. But Leak was terrific, passing for 229 yards, two touchdowns and no interceptions, despite being sacked six times.

Florida's defense also stymied LSU, playing tight and physical in coverage, and smacking LSU's receivers hard every time they touched the ball.

STAFF PHOTO BY ALEX BRANDON

Defensive back Travis Daniels and the Tigers find the game slipping away as Gators running back Ciatrick Fason scores on a 35-yard pass in the third quarter.

But the Tigers said Saturday's loss was not a case of overlooking Florida — which has now beaten LSU in 14 of their past 16 meetings.

If anything was to blame, it might have been LSU's open date last week. The Tigers never lifted the intensity in practice or in the game.

"It seemed like that game was so far away," Clayton said of the two weeks between games.

"You know, even the Tiger Walk didn't have the enthusiasm that it usually has," Saban said of LSU's pregame march

STAFF PHOTO BY ALEX BRANDON

With Skyler Green scoring on an 80-yard punt return in the first quarter to give LSU an early lead, all is right for Tigers fans. But soon after, LSU's magic disappeared.

into the stadium. "You see it every week in college football. This is not anything that hasn't happened every week to two or three teams. And you try to get your team not to be a victim of that by having the right psychological disposition.

"And we just didn't seem to be able to get it on today, for whatever reason."

The mistakes started early for LSU when safety Travis Daniels dropped an interception that might have been a touchdown and a 14-0 lead.

When the Tigers were on offense, Mauck and his receivers couldn't get on the same page. Clayton took the blame for Mauck's first interception — Mauck threw to a place where Clayton was supposed to be, but Clayton had "bailed out" on the route.

Many of Mauck's passes looked like that — they were thrown to a spot with no receiver. He completed 19 of 33 passes for 231 yards, no touchdowns and two interceptions.

"There were a couple times it was basically a read that the receiver didn't go the way I thought he would," Mauck said. "It really hasn't happened all year long. And for some reason today, it just kept happening over and over.

"And it's our fault for not fixing it."

LSU finally had some scoring chances in the fourth quarter. But the Tigers were stopped on fourth-and-two on the Florida 40-yard line when Mauck gained 1 yard on a quarterback keeper.

Also in the fourth, Mauck threw an interception in Florida territory. Later in the quarter, Henderson fumbled at the Florida 31-yard line — LSU's deepest penetration of the game.

"We basically deserved what we got," Saban said. "Now hopefully we're going to learn from it and we'll get better from it. It's just too bad that you have to have a catastrophe happen for people to be willing to listen and learn."

AP TOP 10

RANK, SCHOOL	LAST WEEK
1. OKLAHOMA	1
2. MIAMI (FLA.)	2
3. VIRGINIA TECH	4
4. GEORGIA	8
5. SOUTHERN CAL	9
6. WASHINGTON STATE	12
7. FLORIDA STATE	5
8. OHIO STATE	3
9. IOWA	14
10. LSU	6

Released Oct. 12

FLORIDA	10	3	6	0	19
LSU	7	0	0	0	7

SCORING SUMMARY

LSU Skyler Green 80-yard punt return (Ryan Gaudet kick)

FLORIDA Ran Carthon 22-yard pass from Chris Leak (Matt Leach kick). Thirteen plays, 80 yards in 5:00

FLORIDA Leach 29-yard field goal. Six plays, 18 yards in 1:43

FLORIDA Leach 50-yard field goal. Six plays, 32 yards in 1:58

FLORIDA Ciatrick Fason 35-yard pass from Leak (Leak pass failed). Six plays, 48 yards in 1:58

TEAM STATISTICS

CATEGORY	FLORIDA	LSU
FIRST DOWNS	18	14
RUSHES-YARDS (NET)	40-81	24-56
PASSING YARDS (NET)	229	231
PASSES ATT-COMP-INT	30-18-0	33-19-2
TOTAL OFFENSE PLAYS-YARDS	70-310	57-287
PUNT RETURNS-YARDS	3-43	4-123
KICKOFF RETURNS-YARDS	0-0	2-36
PUNTS (NUMBER-AVG)	7-50.7	8-48.5
FUMBLES-LOST	2-1	2-1
PENALTIES-YARDS	5-41	13-99
POSSESSION TIME	30:20	29:40
SACKS BY (NUMBER-YARDS)	3-18	6-56

INDIVIDUAL OFFENSIVE STATISTICS

RUSHING: **LSU** — Joseph Addai 10-39; Justin Vincent 4-10; Matt Mauck 10-7. **Florida** — Ciatrick Fason 7-92; Ran Carthon 7-35; DeShawn Wynn 10-20; Jimtavis Walker 3-7; team 2 minus-7; Chris Leak 11 minus-66

PASSING: **LSU** — Matt Mauck 19-33-2-231. **Florida** — Chris Leak 18-30-0-229

RECEIVING: **LSU** — Devery Henderson 5-109; Michael Clayton 5-60; Skyler Green 3-29; Joseph Addai 2-8; Justin Vincent 2-8; Demetri Robinson 1-9; Eric Edwards 1-8 **Florida** — O.J. Small 7-50; Carlos Perez 3-58; Ran Carthon 3-37; Kelvin Kight 2-31; Ciatrick Fason 1-35; Ben Troupe 1-16; DeShawn Wynn 1-2

INDIVIDUAL DEFENSIVE STATISTICS

INTERCEPTIONS: **LSU** — none. **Florida** — Keiwan Ratliff 2-45

SACKS (unassisted-assisted): **LSU** — Chad Lavalais 2-0; Travis Daniels 1-0; Kyle Williams 1-0; LaRon Landry 1-0; Marcus Spears 1-0. **Florida** — Bobby McCray 3-0.

TACKLES (unassisted-assisted): **LSU** — Lionel Turner 7-2; LaRon Landry 6-3; Bryce Wyatt 6-0; Eric Alexander 4-2; Chad Lavalais 4-3; Cameron Vaughn 4-2; Marcus Spears 3-2; Travis Daniels 3-2; Corey Webster 3-1. **Florida** — Guss Scott 7-1; Keiwan Ratliff 6-1; Johnny Lamar 5-1; Bobby McCray 4-0

#93 CHAD LAVALAIS

Coach Nick Saban and several LSU players received dozens of postseason honors and awards this season, but no one was honored more often than senior defensive tackle Chad Lavalais.

Lavalais was chosen the Defensive Player of the Year by the Sporting News and was a finalist for the Outland Trophy, the Lombardi Award and the Nagurski Award. He was selected first-team All-American by seven publications, including The Associated Press, Sports Illustrated, the Sporting News and the Football Writers Association of America.

"I knew if I had a full, healthy season, I knew I could put it together," Lavalais said. "It was just a matter of time, just learning the system, learning different techniques to use in the game, getting better with each game."

Lavalais has been a standout at LSU for four years. He earned his first start as a freshman against Alabama, and responded immediately with eight tackles and a sack. By his junior year he was one of the top interior linemen in the Southeastern Conference, equally strong against the run and pass, with the ability to disrupt offenses with excellent leverage and speed.

Yet even Lavalais couldn't have predicted his senior year would be so memorable. And as he found himself in the crowd at the nationally televised College Football Awards, the Marksville native still found it hard to believe.

"I was telling some friends the other day, just being nominated and being mentioned with some of those guys up there and knowing where I came from, I have great appreciation for it. I was like, 'Man, how many people can say they've been through what I've been through?' " — Mike Triplett

FULL NAME: Chad Douglas Lavalais
BORN: Aug. 15, 1979
BIRTHPLACE: Marksville
ATTENDED: Marksville High School
FAMILY: Mother is Carol Lavalais, and brother is Petey
Major: Education
POSITION: Defensive tackle
HEIGHT: 6 feet 3
WEIGHT: 292 pounds

CAREER STATISTICS

YEAR	GAMES	STARTS	TACKLES	ASSISTS	TOTAL	TACKLES FOR LOSS	SACKS
2000	11	3	16	6	22	3	1
2001	11	11	34	19	53	5	1
2002	13	13	43	23	66	8.5	2
2003	14	14	34	27	61	16	7

STAFF PHOTO BY ALEX BRANDON

GAME 7 | OCTOBER 18, 2003

WILLIAMS–BRICE STADIUM | COLUMBIA, S.C.

BACK IN STRIDE

TIGERS REBOUND
TO TRAMPLE SOUTH CAROLINA

LSU wide receiver Devery Henderson scores on a 5-yard touchdown pass in the first quarter against South Carolina. The Tigers never looked back.

AP PHOTO

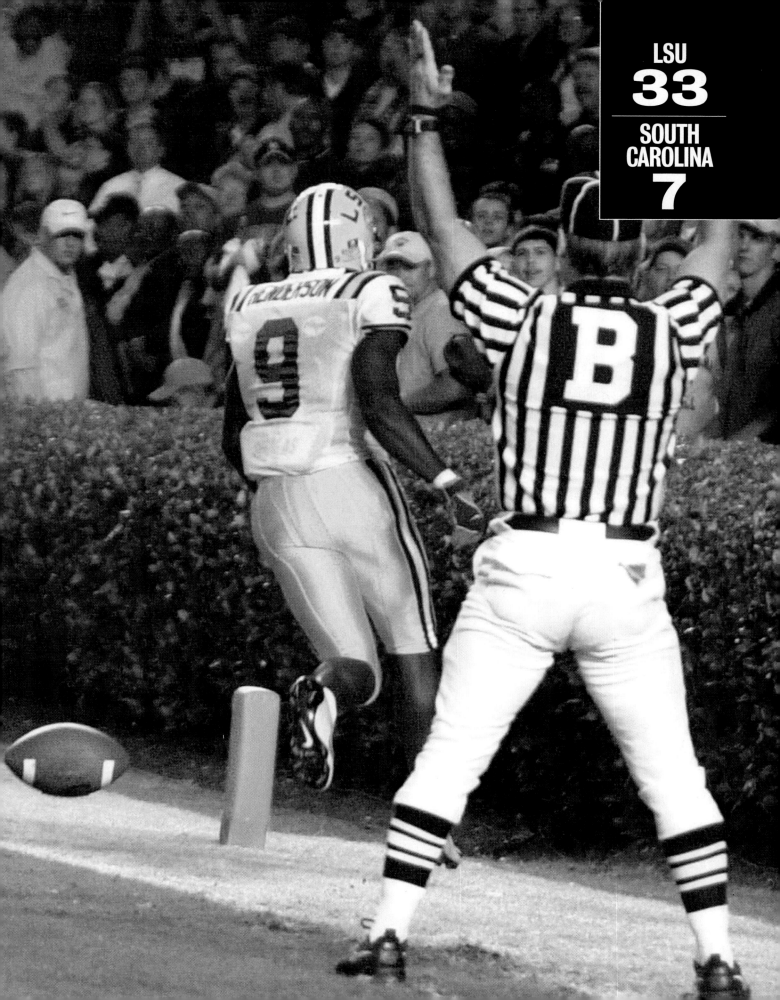

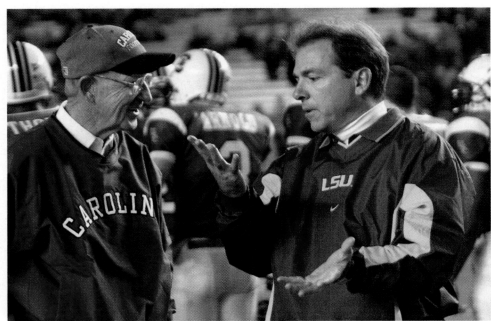

South Carolina coach Lou Holtz is all smiles with LSU coach Nick Saban before the game. Following the Gamecocks' 33-7 setback, Holtz said the Tigers 'outplayed, outcoached and most importantly, out-enthusiasmed' his team.

AP PHOTO

LSU 33
S. CAROLINA 7

LSU OVERWHELMING ON ROAD ONE WEEK AFTER FLORIDA FIASCO

BY MIKE TRIPLETT STAFF WRITER

What a difference a week makes. LSU went from awful to awfully good in a span of seven days, beating South Carolina 33-7 Saturday night.

The win improved LSU to 6-1 overall and 3-1 in the SEC, as they rebounded from a collapse against Florida the previous week.

The Tigers rushed for 263 yards — with their top two tail-backs nursing knee injuries on the sideline. Freshmen Alley Broussard and Justin Vincent combined to gain 185 yards on 35 carries. The Tigers were clearly motivated by last week's loss.

"I'm really proud of our team, bouncing back in a tough place to play," LSU coach Nick Saban said. "It was kind of our goal to come back and re-establish our identity as a team."

LSU was determined to return to form this week, and the Gamecocks just happened to be the poor suckers standing in their way.

The biggest transformation came on offense.

After failing to score an offensive touchdown against the Gators, LSU scored touchdowns on each of its first three possessions against South Carolina. And they were doozies.

The first scoring drive covered 64 yards on eight plays. The second covered 97 yards on 21 plays. And the third went 91 yards on 14 plays.

Meanwhile, LSU's defense did not allow South Carolina to get past the Tigers' 34-yard line in the first half.

"We got outplayed, outcoached and most importantly, out-enthusiasmed," said despondent South Carolina coach Lou Holtz.

The Tigers led 19-0 at halftime despite two missed

AP TOP 10

RANK, SCHOOL	LAST WEEK
1. OKLAHOMA	1
2. MIAMI (FLA.)	2
3. VIRGINIA TECH	3
4. GEORGIA	4
5. SOUTHERN CAL	5
6. WASHINGTON STATE	6
6. FLORIDA STATE	7
8. OHIO STATE	8
9. LSU	10
10. PURDUE	13

Released Oct. 19

BCS RANKINGS

RANK, SCHOOL	TOTAL
1. OKLAHOMA	2.77
2. MIAMI (FLA.)	4.10
3. VIRGINIA TECH	10.23
4. GEORGIA	12.99
5. FLORIDA STATE	13.14
6. OHIO STATE	13.20
7. SOUTHERN CAL	13.83
8. PURDUE	21.50
9. WASHINGTON STATE	23.96
10. NORTHERN ILLINOIS	26.00
12. LSU	26.54

Released Oct. 20

LSU	6	13	7	7	33
S. CAROLINA	0	0	7	0	7

SCORING SUMMARY

LSU Devery Henderson 5-yard pass from Matt Mauck (Ryan Gaudet kick failed). Eight plays, 64 yards in 4:19

LSU Eric Edwards 4-yard pass from Mauck (Gaudet kick). Twenty-one plays, 97 yards in 9:37

LSU Justin Vincent 1-yard run (Mauck rush failed). Fourteen plays, 91 yards in 5:51

SOUTH CAROLINA Matthew Thomas 77-yard pass from Dondrial Pinkins (Daniel Weaver kick). Three plays, 80 yards in 1:33

LSU Jason LeDoux 15-yard fumble recovery (Gaudet kick)

LSU Justin Vincent 1-yard run (Gaudet kick). Ten plays, 62 yards in 4:57

TEAM STATISTICS

CATEGORY	SOUTH CAROLINA	LSU
FIRST DOWNS	11	27
RUSHES-YARDS (NET)	17-0	52-263
PASSING YARDS (NET)	254	219
PASSES ATT-COMP-INT	32-15-0	32-26-1
TOTAL OFFENSE PLAYS-YARDS	49-254	84-482
PUNT RETURNS-YARDS	0-0	0-0
KICKOFF RETURNS-YARDS	6-67	1-18
PUNTS (NUMBER-AVG)	7-38.7	3-36.0
FUMBLES-LOST	1-1	0-0
PENALTIES-YARDS	4-22	7-64
POSSESSION TIME	18:17	41:43
SACKS BY (NUMBER-YARDS)	0-0	0-0

INDIVIDUAL OFFENSIVE STATISTICS

RUSHING: **LSU** — Alley Broussard 19-108; Justin Vincent 16-77; Matt Mauck 4-40; Barrington Edwards 8-37. **South Carolina** — Demetris Summers 8-16; Dondrial Pinkins, 3 minus-26

PASSING: **LSU** — Matt Mauck 24-30-1-199; Marcus Randall 2-2-0-20. **South Carolina** — Dondrial Pinkins 15-32-0-254

RECEIVING: **LSU** — Skyler Green 6-44; Eric Edwards 5-37; Justin Vincent 4-46; David Jones 3-25; Devery Henderson 3-18; Michael Clayton 2-24. **South Carolina** — Matthew Thomas 4-102; Syvelle Newton 3-85

INDIVIDUAL DEFENSIVE STATISTICS

INTERCEPTIONS: **LSU** — none. **South Carolina** — Tremaine Tyler 1-0

SACKS (unassisted-assisted): **LSU** — Kirston Pittman 1-0. **South Carolina** — none

TACKLES (unassisted-assisted): **LSU** — LaRon Landry 5-2; Marcus Spears 4-2; Lionel Turner 2-4; Chad Lavalais 3-2; Jesse Daniels 2-3; Jack Hunt 3-1; Marquise Hill 2-2. **South Carolina** — Jeremiah Garrison 8-2; Jermaine Harris 6-4; Corey Peoples 7-2

conversions, and they held the ball for 19 minutes, 47 seconds of the first half.

"Our offensive line did the best job of the year," Saban said, "but our runners did a good job running the ball. All of them. We wanted to use Justin Vincent and Barrington Edwards as more of our all-purpose guys. But Alley Broussard ran a few plays extremely well, so we stayed with him."

Vincent, who had the most experience of any LSU tailback coming in, started. But Broussard quickly made his presence felt, busting a 33-yard carry on third-and-two to set up LSU's first touchdown. Broussard sprinted around the left side and plowed over safety Rodriques Wilson before being run out of bounds at the 7-yard line. Three plays later, quarterback Matt Mauck passed to Devery Henderson for a 5-yard touchdown.

Broussard rushed for 108 yards on 19 carries. Vincent ran 16 times for 77 yards. Edwards, also a freshman, got into the mix in the fourth quarter, gaining 37 yards on eight carries. Even Mauck had his best rushing performance of the season, carrying four times for 40 yards.

Mauck was equally effective throwing the ball. He completed 24 of 30 passes for 199 yards, two touchdowns and one interception.

"Any time you come on the road, you want to be able to set the tempo and control everything," Mauck said. "And we did that."

'A TOTAL TEAM WIN'

LSU DELIVERS AN EARLY KNOCKOUT IN ONE-SIDED VICTORY

GAME 8 | OCTOBER 25, 2003

TIGER STADIUM | BATON ROUGE

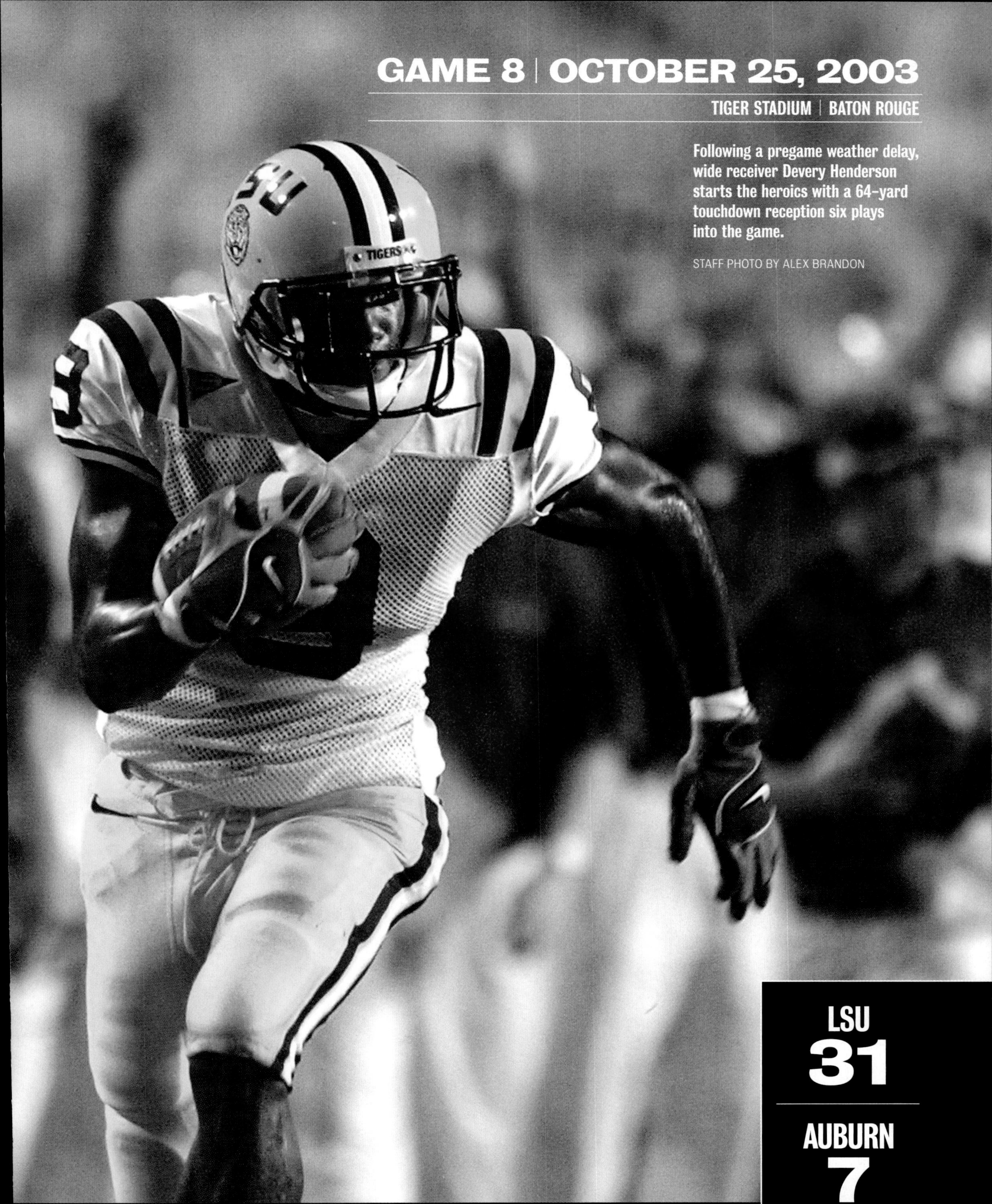

Following a pregame weather delay, wide receiver Devery Henderson starts the heroics with a 64-yard touchdown reception six plays into the game.

STAFF PHOTO BY ALEX BRANDON

LSU
31

AUBURN
7

LSU	31
AUBURN	7

THREE TOUCHDOWNS IN FIRST 12 MINUTES HELP DO THE TRICK

BY MIKE TRIPLETT STAFF WRITER

After a pregame weather delay, LSU's offense struck like lightning.

LSU knocked Auburn silly with a 31-7 victory, its most decisive win over Auburn since a 28-point rout in 1972.

LSU scored three touchdowns in the first 12 minutes, on just 17 plays. It started with a 64-yard touchdown pass from Matt Mauck to Devery Henderson, six plays into the game, and Auburn never recovered.

The win lifted LSU (7-1, 4-1 SEC) to its best start since the 1987 season, when LSU started 8-0-1 en route to a 10-1-1 year.

"I was very proud of the way we played. That was a total team win," LSU coach Nick Saban said. "It was a great atmosphere to play a football game in. The excitement before the game was electric, and I think our players came out and played that way early in the game, which helped us get a jump in the game."

Auburn "is a team that would probably rather play from ahead than from behind. I think that helped us," Saban said.

Auburn coach Tommy Tuberville said the game was like "déjà vu" from last year, when Auburn beat LSU 31-7.

"We got off to a slow start, and the rest is history," Tuberville said. "We got beat up front on both sides of the line, and when you can't control the line of scrimmage on the road, you are in trouble."

Highly touted running back Carnell 'Cadillac' Williams finds there is no room to maneuver as LSU avenges last season's loss to Auburn.

STAFF PHOTO BY ALEX BRANDON

LSU's offense enjoys much success in the first quarter, including quarterback Matt Mauck's 18-yard touchdown pass to wide receiver Michael Clayton, right.

The matchup was billed as a smash-mouth game that would be decided at the line of scrimmage. LSU came in with the nation's No. 1-ranked run defense, and Auburn entered with one of the country's most intimidating rushing offenses.

But LSU took such a big lead so quickly that Auburn was forced to throw for most of the final three quarters.

LSU freshman Justin Vincent was the rushing star, carry-ing 14 times for 127 yards. Auburn's stud, Carnell "Cadillac" Williams, ran for just 61 yards on 20 carries with no touchdowns.

Auburn rushed for just 50 total yards, thanks to LSU's five sacks for minus-47 yards.

"Basically, Auburn runs the ball to the motion. So we loaded up toward the motion guy. Then we struck and hit

STAFF PHOTO BY ALEX BRANDON

Capping off a dominating performance against the Plainsmen in the first quarter, running back Alley Broussard scores on a 5-yard scamper to give LSU a 21-0 lead.

the gap," LSU linebacker Eric Alexander explained. "Our goal was to create a new line of scrimmage. That's why you saw us in the backfield all night."

The biggest surprise Saturday was LSU's dynamic, quick-strike offense.

LSU receivers Michael Clayton and Henderson had been held mostly in check since September. But Henderson caught two touchdown passes on Saturday, and Clayton caught one. Henderson broke free on LSU's opening drive against Auburn's zone defense. Auburn cornerback Junior Rosegreen was caught peeking at Clayton on a slant route, and Henderson burned past him to get open.

Henderson ran untouched for the final 45 yards or so, giving LSU a 7-0 lead less than two minutes into the game.

With coach Tommy Tuberville opting to go for the first down on fourth-and-one, LSU defensive tackle Chad Lavalais sacks Jason Campbell early in the first quarter.

Deciding to go airborne, LSU receiver Michael Clayton isn't satisfied until he scores on an 18-yard reception during the first quarter.

STAFF PHOTOS BY ALEX BRANDON

AP TOP 10

RANK, SCHOOL	LAST WEEK
1. OKLAHOMA	1
2. MIAMI (FLA.)	2
3. SOUTHERN CAL	5
4. GEORGIA	4
5. FLORIDA STATE	6
6. WASHINGTON STATE	6
7. LSU	9
8. OHIO STATE	8
9. MICHIGAN STATE	11
10. VIRGINIA TECH	3

Released Oct. 26

BCS RANKINGS

RANK, SCHOOL	TOTAL
1. OKLAHOMA	2.45
2. MIAMI (FLA.)	3.87
3. FLORIDA STATE	10.34
4. SOUTHERN CAL	11.07
5. GEORGIA	11.15
6. OHIO STATE	12.60
7. LSU	18.68
8. WASHINGTON STATE	20.67
9. NEBRASKA	21.38
10. MICHIGAN STATE	23.53

Released Oct. 27

Clayton caught the next touchdown pass on an 18-yard inside screen play. Tailback Alley Broussard ran in the third touchdown of the first quarter from five yards, giving LSU a 21-0 lead. Henderson's other touchdown came on a 16-yard bullet from Mauck in the third quarter.

"It felt real good to score again. It always feels good to score a touchdown," said Clayton, who had been held out of the end zone since LSU's victory over Western Illinois on Sept. 13. Clayton said the aerial assault was "just an advantage we saw against their style of defense."

LSU's special teams were every bit as effective as the Tigers' offense and defense. LSU forced two fumbles on punt returns in the second quarter. LSU did not score after either fumble, but Saban said it helped LSU control the field position.

LSU's Donnie Jones also boomed a 67-yard punt during the scoreless second quarter, when Auburn failed to get itself back into the game.

LSU punt returner Skyler Green set up LSU's third touchdown with a 44-yard return to the Auburn 28-yard line.

"Special teams did a fantastic job," Saban said. "And our offense did a fantastic job, especially early in the game, creating tremendous momentum for our team."

There was plenty of credit to pass around. Mauck completed 17 of 28 passes, including seven of nine in the first quarter. He threw for 224 yards, three touchdowns and one interception. Defensive tackle Chad Lavalais continued an outstanding senior season with one sack and three tackles for loss.

	1	2	3	4	
AUBURN	0	0	0	7	7
LSU	21	0	10	0	31

SCORING SUMMARY

LSU Devery Henderson 64-yard pass from Matt Mauck (Ryan Gaudet kick). Six plays, 80 yards in 1:59

LSU Michael Clayton 18-yard pass from Mauck (Gaudet kick). Six plays, 52 yards in 1:40

LSU Alley Broussard 5-yard run (Gaudet kick). Five plays, 28 yards in 2:15

LSU Gaudet 33-yard field goal. Seven plays, 42 yards in 3:42

LSU Henderson 16-yard pass from Mauck (Gaudet kick). Six plays, 60 yards in 2:18

AUBURN Anthony Mix 6-yard pass from Jason Campbell (Philip Yost kick). Nine plays, 53 yards in 4:34

TEAM STATISTICS

CATEGORY	AUBURN	LSU
FIRST DOWNS	15	15
RUSHES-YARDS (NET)	34-50	33-157
PASSING YARDS (NET)	143	224
PASSES ATT-COMP-INT	27-19-0	28-17-1
TOTAL OFFENSE PLAYS-YARDS	61-193	61-381
PUNT RETURNS-YARDS	2-1	5-87
KICKOFF RETURNS-YARDS	2-37	0-0
PUNTS (NUMBER-AVG)	7-47.0	5-43.4
FUMBLES-LOST	2-2	1-0
PENALTIES-YARDS	4-15	4-40
POSSESSION TIME	33:41	26:19
SACKS BY (NUMBER-YARDS)	0-0	5-47

INDIVIDUAL OFFENSIVE STATISTICS

RUSHING: **LSU** — Justin Vincent 14-127; Alley Broussard 13-31; Barrington Edwards 2-5; Matt Mauck 3 minus-3. **Auburn** — Carnell Williams 20-61; Ronnie Brown 7-30

PASSING: **LSU** — Matt Mauck 17-28-1-224. **Auburn** — Jason Campbell 19-27-0-143

RECEIVING: **LSU** — Devery Henderson 6-101; Michael Clayton 6-59; Eric Edwards 2-31; Skyler Green 2-18. **Auburn** — Anthony Mix 5-47; Cooper Wallace 4-35; Ben Obomanu 4-24

INDIVIDUAL DEFENSIVE STATISTICS

INTERCEPTIONS: **LSU** — none. **Auburn** — DeMarco McNeil 1-0

SACKS (unassisted-assisted): **LSU** — Kyle Williams 2-0; Chad Lavalais 1-0; Marcus Spears 1-0; Marquise Hill 0-1; Eric Alexander 1-0. **Auburn** — none

TACKLES (unassisted-assisted): **LSU** — Jack Hunt 7-3; LaRon Landry 6-2; Chad Lavalais 6-2; Cameron Vaughn 3-4; Lionel Turner 3-4; Marcus Spears 4-2; Randall Gay 5-0; Eric Alexander 3-2; Corey Webster 4-0; Kyle Williams 3-1. **Auburn** — Karlos Dansby 8-3; Travis Williams 5-4; D. Thomas 6-2; Karibi Dede 5-1

LSU ASSAULTS AUBURN WITH EARLY BARRAGE

BY PETER FINNEY
COLUMNIST

If it had been a prize fight, the referee would have stopped it.

A 12-minute knockout.

But this was football and on they played, a couple of Tigers teams, for a full 60 minutes, at which time LSU left Auburn for dead in Death Valley.

Dead as 31-7.

Dead as someone staggered by some early body shots and unable to recover.

Dead as someone who showed up full of swagger, only to depart more than a little punch-drunk.

What Nick Saban's football team did was fashion its most impressive victory of a 7-1 season that has his Tigers in control of their destiny in the SEC West.

This was an Auburn club some pundits picked to win the national championship. It was a talented bunch that had settled down after a rocky start and arrived in Tiger Stadium confident of making a statement.

It had the makings of a fierce battle.

Well, what a crowd of 92,085 saw was more of a mismatch, more a case of superbly prepared LSU making it pretty much an evening of 1-2-3 and you're out.

Auburn was never in it. LSU wouldn't allow it. It was 7-0 after two minutes, 14-0 after seven minutes, 21-0 after 12 minutes.

It was this kind of evening for the losers. Freshman Justin

Vincent outrushed All-America candidate Carnell "Cadillac" Williams 127-61. Williams, who came in on the wings of three consecutive 100-yards-plus outings, squeezed through every bit of daylight he could find, which wasn't much, as LSU clawed at him in a gang-tackling mode that left him many times under a pile of white shirts.

Offensively, Matt Mauck went to battle with a crisp run-pass plan that kept Auburn off-balance and, at times, bewildered.

"Matt did a great job of check-with-me," Saban said of a flock of audibles that kept producing real estate, on the ground and in the air. His most crucial completion, one that set the tenor of the game, was his 64-yard hookup with Devery Henderson, the first of three touchdown passes by a quarterback fully in control.

"We got an early jump and we never lost focus," Saban said. "On the defensive end, we got some big plays from Chad Lavalais. But this was a total team win, the kind you need against a team like Auburn."

With two exceptions, Saban could not have sat at his desk and scripted a more dreamy first half.

Mauck came out throwing and thinking. After moving the Tigers from the 20 to the 36, he faced a third-and-five. Auburn called a timeout as LSU lined up, fearing it was in the wrong defense. When play resumed, Mauck obviously liked what he saw. And he knew immediately where he was going with the football. Michael Clayton, on the outside, and Henderson, on the inside, proceeded to run a crisscross pattern that gave Henderson all the daylight he needed as he converted a soft lob from his quarterback into a 64-yard score.

And there was more coming.

On Auburn's first series, coach Tommy Tuberville took a huge gamble on fourth-and-one at his 29, and Williams converted. Moments later, with Auburn on the LSU 43, Tuberville took another fourth-and-one gamble, but this time Lavalais rode Williams down five yards behind the line as Tiger Stadium exploded. Six plays later, it was 14-0 when Mauck, on a third-and-eight at the 18, hooked up with Clayton on a quick move over the middle that ended with Clayton shaking one tackler on his way to a dive into the end zone.

It wasn't over.

There was Lavalais coming up with another big play — a sack for minus-13 yards that forced a punt. And there was

STAFF PHOTO BY ALEX BRANDON

LSU's defense, including linebacker Lionel Turner (58), makes life miserable for receiver Anthony Mix during the second quarter.

Skyler Green coming up with another one, a 44-yard punt return to the Auburn 28. Five plays later, Alley Broussard was bouncing in to make it 21-0.

In the second quarter, LSU had two chances to widen the gap when it recovered fumbled punts, one at the Auburn 29, another at the 31. But LSU came up empty, first on a missed field-goal attempt from 50 yards, later on an interception of a Mauck pass.

The final 30 minutes was a matter of LSU remaining confident and in complete control.

"We have no excuses," said Tuberville, who is 2-2 against Saban. "They lined up and whipped us on both sides of the ball. When you can't control the line of scrimmage, you're in trouble."

For Auburn, that's where the trouble began. And that's where this game ended.

#14 MICHAEL CLAYTON

LSU coach Nick Saban constantly is reminding his players how important it is not to look past the next play or the next game. When he needs a model for the players, he can point to junior wide receiver Michael Clayton.

No player exhibits more focus and intensity play after play, according to Saban. That was apparent when Clayton caught a career-high 12 passes for 130 yards and a touchdown in the Tigers' 27-3 victory against Alabama on Nov. 15.

Despite dropping one potential touchdown pass and losing a fumble, Clayton contributed in many areas. He had a crushing block on a key 27-yard pass play as Skyler Green wove his way through the Alabama defense, and had a tackle on special teams.

"It always seems that, no matter what the circumstance or situation, he seems to be able to (focus) fairly well," Saban said.

Clayton said it's a trait he has picked up since coming to LSU.

"I remember making mistakes as a freshman and letting it upset me," Clayton said. "When you see the outcome of putting it behind you and moving to the next play, it becomes natural. It's something I've polished over the years."

Clayton, a consensus high school All-American, is a tremendous athlete who can play both sides of the football, gaining much attention for his performance on offense and defense against Texas in the Cotton Bowl during his sophomore season.

But being cast into the spotlight came early for Clayton, who — as a freshman — was part of a one-two receiving corps with Josh Reed that blistered the Southeastern Conference during a championship run and domination of Illinois in the Sugar Bowl.

Said Saban: Clayton's "a great leader, he's got tremendous character as a person, which affects people, and he makes plays."

What more could Tigers fans want? — Jim Kleinpeter

NAME: Michael Rashard Clayton
BORN: Oct. 13, 1982
BIRTHPLACE: Baton Rouge
ATTENDED: Christian Life Academy
FAMILY: Parents are Milton and Marjorie Clayton. Has two brothers, Milton and Marcus, and one sister, Marcie
MAJOR: Communications
POSITION: Wide receiver
HEIGHT: 6 feet 4
WEIGHT: 200 pounds

CAREER STATISTICS

YEAR	GAMES	STARTS	REC.	YARDS	TDS
2001	12	4	47	754	6
2002	13	13	57	749	5
2003	14	14	78	1,079	10

LSU
49

LA. TECH
10

TECH-NICAL KNOCKOUT

TIGERS' ROUT OF LOUISIANA TECH COMES AT AN OPPORTUNE TIME

GAME 9 | NOVEMBER 1, 2003

TIGER STADIUM | BATON ROUGE

LSU's defense does its best to help out with the scoring, and safety Jack Hunt obliges with a 29-yard interception return for a touchdown in the first quarter.

STAFF PHOTO
BY MICHAEL DEMOCKER

LSU	49
LA. TECH	10

SABAN EMPHASIZES IT'S TOO EARLY TO TALK TITLE

BY MIKE TRIPLETT STAFF WRITER

On a day when three top 10 teams lost, LSU got a break in the schedule and took full advantage, beating up on Louisiana Tech 49-10.

No. 2 Miami lost. So did No. 4 Georgia and No. 6 Washington State.

If LSU coach Nick Saban didn't want to talk about his Tigers being in contention for the national championship before, he'd have to now, with LSU ranked in the top five for the first time since 1987.

Right?

Uh, no.

"I have zero concern about it. Zero," Saban said, downplaying the rankings. "Because none of that matters unless we win the games that we play, and we've got three games left.

"I don't even know where Washington State is. How do I have anything to do with whether they win or lose? All I can do is something about our guys winning or losing, and that's what we're going to try to do."

First things first. LSU (8-1, 4-1 SEC) needs to win the SEC's Western Division. That likely will require running the table against Alabama and Ole Miss on the road and Arkansas at home, following this week's bye.

LSU keeps rolling on offense, amassing 653 yards — including wide receiver Michael Clayton's 34-yard touchdown reception in the first quarter — against Louisiana Tech.

STAFF PHOTO BY MICHAEL DEMOCKER

STAFF PHOTO BY MICHAEL DeMOCKER

Tackling by committee is the preferred method with the Tigers, as Bulldogs running back Ryan Moats learns firsthand.

But if Saturday night is any indication, the Tigers look like a team that is gaining steam as it heads into the stretch run.

"That was just a fantastic football team we played. If they are not the best team in the country, I'd be shocked," Louisiana Tech coach Jack Bicknell said. "We played Miami, and I promise you, I feel like they are better than Miami."

The Tigers suffered their only loss to Florida on Oct. 11 because they came out flat and unemotional. Since then, LSU has been a team on a mission.

The Tigers gained 653 yards against Tech, the most since they racked up 680 against Western Carolina in 2000.

"The way we're playing right now is how I visualized we were capable of playing, and we wanted to get to be able to play," Saban said.

LSU led 28-0 in the first quarter and 49-3 before half-time. Tigers quarterback Matt Mauck completed all 14 of his passes in the first half and matched a school record with four touchdown passes in one game.

He connected with Michael Clayton, Skyler Green and Devery Henderson twice. And he did it in the first 20 minutes.

"You look at all the threats that we throw out there," Clayton said. "We have guys like Devery and Skyler who can

AP TOP 10		
RANK, SCHOOL		LAST WEEK
1. OKLAHOMA		1
2. SOUTHERN CAL		3
3. FLORIDA STATE		5
4. LSU		7
5. VIRGINIA TECH		10
6. MIAMI (FLA.)		2
7. OHIO STATE		8
8. MICHIGAN		11
9. GEORGIA		4
10. IOWA		13
Released Nov. 2		

BCS RANKINGS	
RANK, SCHOOL	TOTAL
1. OKLAHOMA	2.24
2. SOUTHERN CAL	7.02
3. FLORIDA STATE	9.52
4. MIAMI (FLA.)	10.25
5. OHIO STATE	11.47
6. VIRGINIA TECH	12.47
7. LSU	14.92
8. MICHIGAN	20.79
9. TCU	24.75
10. GEORGIA	25.15
Released Nov. 3	

make big plays. You can see how explosive we are when everybody gets their touches."

Louisiana Tech has featured the most prolific passing attack in the country the past seven years. But on Saturday, LSU displayed its own firepower, taking advantage of Tech's passing defense, which ranks last in Division I-A.

Mauck found a wide-open Clayton running down the left sideline for a 34-yard touchdown on the Tigers' fourth play from scrimmage.

He hit Green with an 8-yard strike for LSU's third touchdown. And in the second quarter, Mauck threw touchdown passes of 46 and 50 yards to a wide-open Henderson.

"It went real well," said Mauck, who has 19 touchdown passes this season and needs four more to set a school record. "A lot of times the quarterback gets a lot of the credit when he doesn't deserve it, and he gets a lot of the blame when he doesn't deserve it. All my teammates made it easy for me tonight."

LSU's defense was its usual stingy self, except for some brief lapses. Tech scored its only touchdown on a 49-yard pass from Luke McCown to Eric Newman in the third quarter.

In the second quarter, Bulldogs tailback Ryan Moats broke loose for a 60-yard gain. He finished with 124 yards on 16 carries, the most anyone has gained against LSU this season. LSU's tailbacks kept up a hot streak, combining for 281 rushing yards.

LA. TECH	0	3	7	0	10
LSU	28	21	0	0	49

SCORING SUMMARY

LSU Michael Clayton 34-yard pass from Matt Mauck (Ryan Gaudet kick). Four plays, 65 yards in 1:15

LSU Justin Vincent 7-yard run (Gaudet kick). Eight plays, 96 yards in 3:20

LSU Skyler Green 8-yard pass from Mauck (Gaudet kick). Three plays, 20 yards in 59 seconds

LSU Jack Hunt 29-yard interception return (Gaudet kick)

LSU Devery Henderson 46-yard pass from Mauck (Gaudet kick). Three plays, 80 yards in 30 seconds

LA. TECH Josh Scobee 29-yard field goal. Seven plays, 80 yards in 2:40

LSU Henderson 50-yard pass from Mauck (Gaudet kick). Six plays, 80 yards in 2:29

LSU Alley Broussard 22-yard run (Gaudet kick). Six plays, 66 yards in 2:22

LA. TECH Eric Newman, 49-yard pass from Luke McCown (Scobee kick). Four plays, 71 yards in 1:05

TEAM STATISTICS

CATEGORY	LOUISIANA TECH	LSU
FIRST DOWNS	13	27
RUSHES-YARDS (NET)	25-121	41-281
PASSING YARDS (NET)	220	372
PASSES ATT-COMP-INT	39-16-2	31-25-0
TOTAL OFFENSE PLAYS-YARDS	64-341	72-653
PUNT RETURNS-YARDS	2-11	0-0
KICKOFF RETURNS-YARDS	8-141	0-0
PUNTS (NUMBER-AVG)	7-37.4	3-40.7
FUMBLES-LOST	0-0	1-1
PENALTIES-YARDS	8-61	11-83
POSSESSION TIME	27:17	32:43
SACKS BY (NUMBER-YARDS)	0-0	3-20

INDIVIDUAL OFFENSIVE STATISTICS
RUSHING: **LSU** — Alley Broussard 16-106; Barrington Edwards 11-66; Justin Vincent 4-47; Joseph Addai 8-44. **La. Tech** — Ryan Moats 16-124; Danny Wilson 3-1; Luke McCown 3-0.

PASSING: **LSU** — Matt Mauck 18-20-0-311; Marcus Randall 7-10-0-61; Michael Clayton 0-1-0-0. **La. Tech** — Luke McCown 11-28-2-152; Maxie Causey 5-11-0-68

RECEIVING: **LSU** — Skyler Green 9-103; Craig Davis 5-42; Michael Clayton 4-85; D. Henderson 2-96. **La. Tech** — Freddie King 3-77

INDIVIDUAL DEFENSIVE STATISTICS
INTERCEPTIONS: **LSU** — Jack Hunt 1-29; Kyle Williams 1-0. **La. Tech** — none

SACKS (unassisted-assisted): **LSU** — Brian West 2-0; LaRon Landry 1-0

TACKLES (unassisted-assisted): **LSU** — LaRon Landry 6-2; Marcus Spears 4-1; Kyle Williams 4-1; Randall Gay 3-2; Ronnie Prude 3-2; Corey Webster 4-0. **La. Tech** — Byron Santiago 3-5; Antonio Crow 3-4

LSU
27

ALABAMA
3

Coach Nick Saban isn't pleased with the call, but the Tigers' intensity and attitude against the Crimson Tide leaves him in a better mood following the victory.

STAFF PHOTO BY ALEX BRANDON

BUSINESS TRIP

TIGERS SHOW THEY BELONG WITH NATION'S ELITE BY WHIPPING ALABAMA

With LSU's offense in high gear, wide receiver Devery Henderson, who finished with five catches for 68 yards, gets into the act with a reception in the first quarter.

STAFF PHOTO
BY ALEX BRANDON

LSU 27
ALABAMA 3

CAUTIOUS SABAN PROUD OF HIS PLAYERS' INTENSITY

BY MIKE TRIPLETT STAFF WRITER

Against the Alabama Crimson Tide, LSU showed it was time for everyone to stop trying to figure out the BCS and start watching the Tigers.

LSU, it seems, has just begun to fight. While other top-ranked teams are slipping, LSU is rising.

A commanding 27-3 victory over Alabama at Bryant-Denny Stadium was the Tigers' best example yet.

"We made a statement. But the statement ain't finished yet," LSU linebacker Lionel Turner said. "We just have to finish up the season strong, and our statement will be made then."

True, LSU (9-1, 5-1 SEC) has been short on "quality victories" this season and has played a rather diluted schedule. As a result, the Tigers rank fourth in the computer-driven BCS standings.

But that is beginning to change. The Tigers' two most recent conference victories — against Auburn and at Alabama — began a string of LSU's most convincing victories of the season.

If LSU continues to play at this level, the computers and pollsters alike might begin to take notice.

Defensive tackle Chad Lavalais (93), intercepting a pass during the second quarter, and LSU's defense are a tough assignment — just ask Alabama.

STAFF PHOTO BY ALEX BRANDON

STAFF PHOTO BY ALEX BRANDON

Skyler Green takes flight, but the Tigers stayed the course through the air and on the ground against the Crimson Tide.

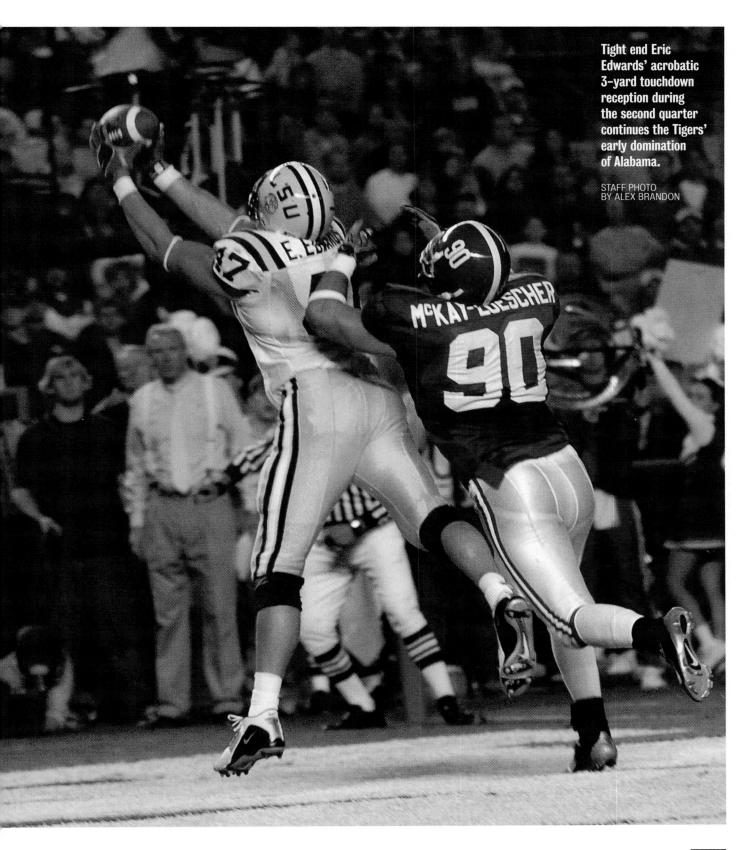

Tight end Eric Edwards' acrobatic 3-yard touchdown reception during the second quarter continues the Tigers' early domination of Alabama.

STAFF PHOTO
BY ALEX BRANDON

STAFF PHOTO BY ALEX BRANDON

Wide receiver Michael Clayton (14) and quarterback Matt Mauck (18) find success early, hooking up on a 23-yard touchdown in the first quarter.

"If Oklahoma is No. 1, they are definitely right behind them," said Alabama coach Mike Shula, whose Crimson Tide lost to the top-ranked Sooners 20-13 in September.

LSU coach Nick Saban was not nearly as enamored with his team Saturday night, complaining about his offense's failure to seal the deal late in the game.

But Saban said he was proud of the intensity and attitude with which LSU began the game. The Tigers were coming off of a bye week, but they picked up right where they left off from a momentum standpoint. LSU has won four straight games — by at least 24 points each.

"I was pleased with the way our players focused on what they needed to focus on in terms of competing and what matters right now," Saban said. "Which was this game and not all the other stuff people like to talk about."

Saban continued to chide the media for talking about the

BCS and national title possibilities. He said he doesn't want his players thinking about that stuff.

"There is nothing at stake," Saban said. "When you act like something is at stake, that is when you mess up, when you create expectations and anxiety. Our worst enemy now is expectations.

"I know y'all would like to mess that up, but you ain't going to do it."

The Tigers clearly did not wilt under the pressure of expectations Saturday. They immediately came out firing on all cylinders.

LSU scored on its first two offensive possessions — first a field goal, then a touchdown — and did not allow Alabama to gain a first down in the first quarter.

The Crimson Tide did not score until settling for a 27-yard field goal with 6:39 remaining to avoid the shutout. A

AP TOP 10

RANK, SCHOOL	LAST WEEK
1. OKLAHOMA	1
2. SOUTHERN CAL	2
3. LSU	3
4. OHIO STATE	4
5. MICHIGAN	5
6. GEORGIA	7
7. TEXAS	6
8. WASHINGTON STATE	8
9. TENNESSEE	9
10. TCU	10

Released Nov. 16

BCS RANKINGS

RANK, SCHOOL	TOTAL
1. OKLAHOMA	1.80
2. OHIO STATE	7.52
3. SOUTHERN CAL	7.71
4. LSU	12.21
5. TEXAS	16.35
6. GEORGIA	16.73
7. TENNESSEE	18.15
8. TCU	19.27
9. MICHIGAN	19.73
10. WASHINGTON STATE	21.03

Released Nov. 17

27-3 victory was still sweet revenge for the Tigers, who lost to Alabama 31-0 in Baton Rouge last year.

Twice, Alabama got inside LSU's 6-yard line. But the Crimson Tide was denied touchdowns both times. And twice, LSU turned the ball over. But LSU's defense immediately responded by forcing Alabama to go three-and-out.

"Woooh. That's real satisfying," LSU defensive tackle Chad Lavalais said of the eight three-and-outs forced by the LSU defense. "Knowing that you go in there, and just three-and-out, bam. Get the ball right back to your offense."

LSU improved its scoring defense — the best in the nation — to 8.6 points allowed per game. The Tigers allowed just 65 rushing yards and held Alabama tailback Shaud Williams to a season-low 29 rushing yards.

Alabama quarterback Brodie Croyle threw for a season-low 154 yards and was sacked twice. LSU missed some opportunities on offense, but the Tigers started and finished strong.

Quarterback Matt Mauck hit Michael Clayton with a 23-yard touchdown pass in the first quarter to give LSU a 10-0 lead. Mauck and Clayton connected nine times in the first half and 12 times overall for 130 yards.

Mauck threw a 3-yard touchdown pass to tight end Eric Edwards in the second quarter. He completed 24 of 36 passes for 251 yards with one interception.

Justin Vincent led the Tigers' four-man rushing attack with 83 yards on 16 carries. Alley Broussard ran for 79 yards and a touchdown on 11 carries.

LSU	10	7	7	3	27
ALABAMA	0	0	0	3	3

SCORING SUMMARY

LSU Chris Jackson 20-yard field goal. Ten plays, 46 yards in 3:24

LSU Michael Clayton 23-yard pass from Matt Mauck (Jackson kick). One play, 23 yards in 6 seconds

LSU Eric Edwards 3-yard pass from Mauck (Jackson kick). Nine plays, 55 yards in 4:00

LSU Alley Broussard 4-yard run (Jackson kick). Nine plays, 72 yards in 3:52

LSU Jackson 33-yard field goal. Eight plays, 67 yards in 3:48

ALABAMA Brian Bostick 27-yard field goal. Ten plays, 75 yards in 3:32

TEAM STATISTICS

CATEGORY	ALABAMA	LSU
FIRST DOWNS	10	28
RUSHES-YARDS (NET)	26-65	40-219
PASSING YARDS (NET)	154	251
PASSES ATT-COMP-INT	33-12-1	36-24-1
TOTAL OFFENSE PLAYS-YARDS	59-219	76-470
PUNT RETURNS-YARDS	2-2	4-69
KICKOFF RETURNS-YARDS	3-78	2-19
PUNTS (NUMBER-AVG)	9-36.3	4-32.8
FUMBLES-LOST	1-0	2-1
PENALTIES-YARDS	5-35	4-42
POSSESSION TIME	25:30	34:30
SACKS BY (NUMBER-YARDS)	0-0	2-15

INDIVIDUAL OFFENSIVE STATISTICS

RUSHING: **LSU** — Justin Vincent 16-83; Alley Broussard 11-79; Joseph Addai 5-31; Matt Mauck 1-16; Shyrone Carey 5-9. **Alabama** — Kenneth Darby 10-41; Shaud Williams 11-29; Brodie Croyle 5 minus-5

PASSING: **LSU** — Matt Mauck 24-36-1-251. **Alabama** — Brodie Croyle 12-33-1-154

RECEIVING: **LSU** — Michael Clayton 12-130; Devery Henderson 5-68; Skyler Green 4-41. **Alabama** — Triandos Luke 4-60

INDIVIDUAL DEFENSIVE STATISTICS

INTERCEPTIONS: **LSU** — Chad Lavalais 1 minus-5. **Alabama** — Charlie Peprah 1-36

SACKS (unassisted-assisted): **LSU** — Melvin Oliver 1-0; Marquise Hill 1-0. **Alabama** — none

TACKLES (unassisted-assisted): **LSU** — LaRon Landry 6-2; Kyle Williams 4-2; Marquise Hill 4-2; Chad Lavalais 3-3; Cameron Vaughn 2-3. **Alabama** — Charlie Peprah 13-1; Derrick Pope 6-3; Anthony Madison 7-0

#13 COREY WEBSTER

One of the most talented and athletic players on the Tigers' squad, cornerback Corey Webster hasn't disappointed this season. With seven interceptions in 2003, he is now second in school history with 14 in his career.

None was bigger than his interception in the final minute against Georgia that sealed LSU's crucial 17-10 victory Sept. 20 at Tiger Stadium. Webster tipped David Greene's pass away from Reggie Brown and was able to secure the ball.

NAME: Corey Jonas Webster
BORN: March 2, 1982
BIRTHPLACE: Vacherie
ATTENDED: St. James High School
FAMILY: Parents are MacArthur and Lorraine Webster. Two sisters, Courtney and Chandra
MAJOR: Business administration
POSITION: Cornerback
HEIGHT: 6 feet
WEIGHT: 201 pounds

"I was reading his eyes down the field, and when he started to go for the ball I turned around because I knew it was coming, and I had to make a play on it," said Webster, who played on offense as a redshirt freshman.

"One of Corey's biggest things coming to defense is learning the intensity you had to play with every play, that you could never be casual," LSU coach Nick Saban said. "He's done a much better job of that, playing with consistency the entire year."

In the regular-season finale against Arkansas, Webster had two interceptions in the Tigers' SEC West-clinching victory. It was sweet revenge for Webster, who was burned by the Razorbacks in 2002 on a 50-yard completion that helped set up Arkansas' winning touchdown in the final seconds — and denying LSU a return trip to the SEC championship game.

"I just wanted to come out and, any way I could, help us get a win; that's what I wanted to do," said Webster, who has received numerous postseason honors for his play this season. "We didn't want the same feeling we had after last year's game."

Webster saw to it they didn't. — Jim Kleinpeter

CAREER STATISTICS

YEAR	GAMES	STARTS	TACKLES	ASSISTS	TOTAL	TACKLES FOR LOSS	INT.
2001*	12	0	(7 CATCHES FOR 74 YARDS ON OFFENSE)				
2002	13	5	31	5	36	1-4	7
2003	14	14	36	10	46	3.5-13	7

*PREDOMINATELY PLAYED ON OFFENSE

STAFF PHOTO BY ALEX BRANDON

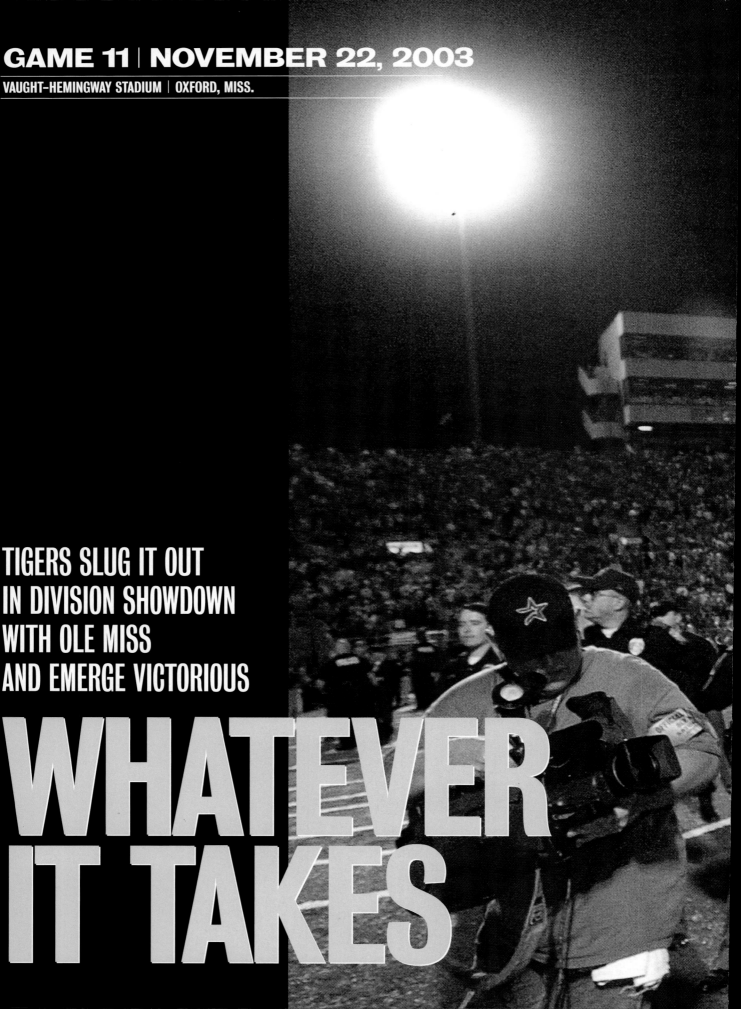

GAME 11 | **NOVEMBER 22, 2003**

VAUGHT–HEMINGWAY STADIUM | OXFORD, MISS.

TIGERS SLUG IT OUT
IN DIVISION SHOWDOWN
WITH OLE MISS
AND EMERGE VICTORIOUS

WHATEVER
IT TAKES

Defensive end Marcus Spears and the Tigers leave the field with only Arkansas standing in their way of capturing the SEC West.

STAFF PHOTO
BY ALEX BRANDON

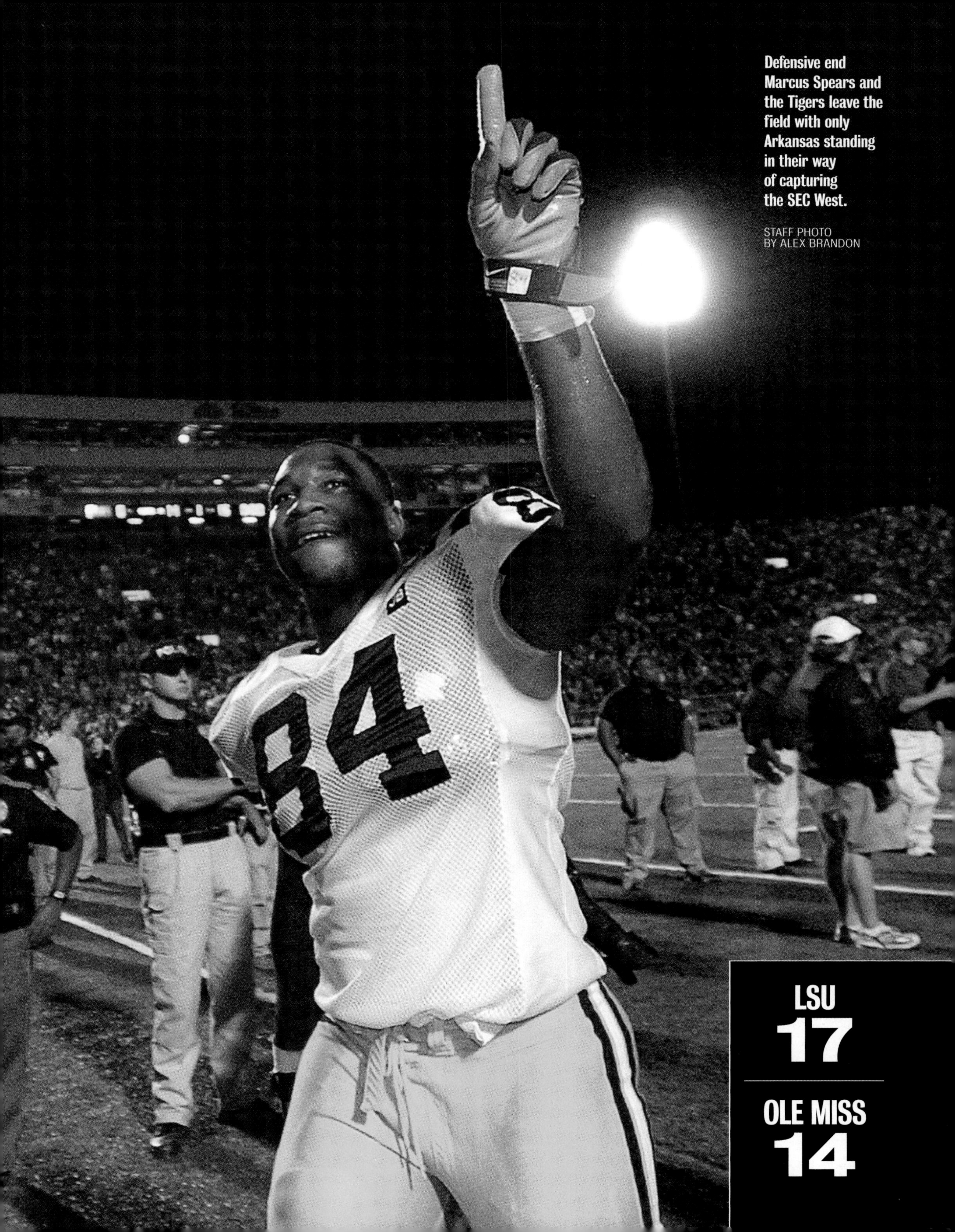

LSU
17

OLE MISS
14

With LSU trailing 7–3, wide receiver Michael Clayton gets the Tigers back in the driver's seat with a 9-yard touchdown reception just before halftime.

STAFF PHOTO BY ALEX BRANDON

LSU 17
OLE MISS 14

LSU IS SOLIDLY IN BCS PICTURE AFTER DIFFICULT WIN

BY MIKE TRIPLETT STAFF WRITER

LSU did what just about every team must do on its way to a national title — the Tigers struggled against a quality team, and they won anyway.

LSU ended its string of dominating performances, but the Tigers found a way to hand a solid Ole Miss team its first conference loss in a 17-14 win at Vaught-Hemingway Stadium.

And this would go down as the week third-ranked LSU officially moved into strong contention for a national championship, thanks to its win and No. 5 Michigan's decisive victory over Ohio State, which came into the week ranked No. 2 in the Bowl Championship Series rankings. The Buckeyes' loss left only Oklahoma, Southern Cal and LSU fighting for the two spots in the Nokia Sugar Bowl.

In a battle of the SEC West's top two teams, LSU left Oxford needing only a win over Arkansas in the regular-season finale to win the division.

"To be honest with you, you almost feel that it's a shame that anybody had to lose. But you've got to be relieved that we were able to come away with a 'W,'" LSU coach Nick Saban said. "I think sometimes it helps that the ball bounces in your direction, whatever you call that. But I think also, the way you compete in a game makes it bounce your way.

"Our defensive players went in there time and time again and made plays when they had to."

LSU's LaRon Landry reacts after Jonathan Nichols (86) missed a 36-yard field-goal attempt late in the fourth quarter with the Rebels trailing 17-14.

STAFF PHOTO BY ALEX BRANDON

The Tigers' offense struggled at the start, but it was good enough in the end. LSU quarterback Matt Mauck threw three interceptions, including one on his first throw of the game that was returned for a touchdown.

That impenetrable Tigers defense showed signs of wear in the fourth quarter, allowing Rebels quarterback Eli Manning to throw a late touchdown pass and put his team in position for a tying field goal.

But Ole Miss kicker Jonathan Nichols missed a 36-yard attempt with 4:15 remaining to seal the Rebels' fate.

An ugly win? Maybe. But it's important for a good team to win on an off day.

"I mean, Ohio State just kept winning all last year," LSU receiver Michael Clayton said of the 2002 national champion, which made a habit of winning close games. "I'm not sure if they were winning ugly or whatever, but a win is a win."

LSU's performance was a near replica of its only loss this season — a 19-7 defeat against Florida six weeks ago. But this time, the Tigers (10-1, 6-1 SEC) rallied after an atrocious start.

Mauck overthrew Clayton on a simple rollout pass on the Tigers' first play, and Ole Miss cornerback Travis Johnson returned it six yards for a touchdown and a 7-0 Rebels lead just 1:06 into the game.

Mauck threw another interception in the second quarter, but the Tigers' defense kept them in the game until Mauck and Clayton finally hooked up for a 9-yard touchdown pass and a 10-7 lead just before halftime.

LSU went ahead 17-7 on Mauck's 53-yard touchdown pass to Devery Henderson early in the fourth quarter.

"I think offensively, maybe we started to press a little bit, myself included," Mauck said. "But our defense just did such a great job and bailed us out every time."

Ole Miss' offense did not score until Manning threw a 10-yard touchdown pass to Brandon Jacobs with 10:51 remaining.

The Rebels got into field-goal range twice, but Nichols missed from 47 yards and 36 yards. He had missed just once all season.

Manning, who would go on to finish third in the Heisman Trophy voting, probably lost his chance to win the award in this game. He finished 16 of 36 for 200 yards with one

STAFF PHOTO BY ALEX BRANDON

After the Rebels grabbed an early 7-0 lead in the first quarter, Tigers wide receiver Michael Clayton, who finished with nine catches for 83 yards, tries to break into the clear.

AP TOP 10

RANK, SCHOOL	LAST WEEK
1. OKLAHOMA	1
2. SOUTHERN CAL	2
3. LSU	3
4. MICHIGAN	5
5. GEORGIA	6
6. TEXAS	7
7. TENNESSEE	9
8. OHIO STATE	4
9. FLORIDA STATE	11
10. MIAMI (FLA.)	13

Released Nov. 23

BCS RANKINGS

RANK, SCHOOL	TOTAL
1. OKLAHOMA	1.90
2. SOUTHERN CAL	6.89
3. LSU	9.04
4. MICHIGAN	10.25
5. OHIO STATE	14.57
6. TEXAS	14.98
7. GEORGIA	15.06
8. TENNESSEE	17.97
9. FLORIDA STATE	21.76
10. MIAMI (FLA.)	22.19

Released Nov. 24

touchdown and one interception.

Manning, a New Orleans native and the son of former Ole Miss and NFL great Archie Manning, had one last chance to rally his Rebels with 2:16 remaining. But he threw three incomplete passes, then tripped over a guard on fourth-and-10, sealing Ole Miss' fate.

"I kind of thought, 'I hope (LSU's offense) throws another interception so we can go out there and stop them again.' Hey, put it on our shoulders," LSU defensive tackle Chad Lavalais said. "It's been on our shoulders all year, so it was no different in this game."

Lavalais took offense when he was asked about some of the Tigers' lucky breaks.

"Luck? This game?" Lavalais said. "The defense has been doing this all year. I see this as the defense stepping up to the challenge."

Saban has tried exhaustively to keep the Tigers from giving in to the pressure of their high expectations. In that respect, he didn't necessarily view the Ole Miss game as a success.

"I didn't think we had our personality today, for whatever reasons," Saban said. "As much as we preached about it, there was a lot of anxiety. We didn't look like ourselves.

"I did everything that we could do to try to get the players to focus on what they needed to do to execute and play good football and not worry about the emotional aspects of what's at stake and all that kind of stuff. When we've done that in two games this year, we haven't played very well."

LSU	3	7	0	7	17
OLE MISS	7	0	0	7	14

SCORING SUMMARY

OLE MISS Travis Johnson 6-yard interception return (Jonathan Nichols kick)

LSU Chris Jackson 45-yard field goal. Fifteen plays, 52 yards in 7:10

LSU Michael Clayton 9-yard pass from Matt Mauck (Jackson kick). Six plays, 71 yards in 2:31

LSU Devery Henderson 53-yard pass from Mauck (Jackson kick). Five plays, 69 yards in 1:03

OLE MISS Brandon Jacobs 10-yard pass from Eli Manning (Nichols kick). Nine plays, 76 yards in 3:59

TEAM STATISTICS

CATEGORY	OLE MISS	LSU
FIRST DOWNS	10	18
RUSHES-YARDS (NET)	21-27	47-152
PASSING YARDS (NET)	200	189
PASSES ATT-COMP-INT	36-16-1	29-16-3
TOTAL OFFENSE PLAYS-YARDS	57-227	76-341
PUNT RETURNS-YARDS	4-37	3-26
KICKOFF RETURNS-YARDS	4-72	2-45
PUNTS (NUMBER-AVG)	8-43.4	7-50.1
FUMBLES-LOST	0-0	0-0
PENALTIES-YARDS	10-70	4-30
POSSESSION TIME	24:11	35:49
SACKS BY (NUMBER-YARDS)	3-37	3-18

INDIVIDUAL OFFENSIVE STATISTICS

RUSHING: **LSU** — Justin Vincent 22-105; Joseph Addai 6-36; Shyrone Carey 6-11. **Ole Miss** — Tremaine Turner 7-27; Vashon Pearson 9-24; Eli Manning 4-minus 23

PASSING: **LSU** — Matt Mauck 16-29-3-189. **Ole Miss** — Eli Manning 16-36-1-200

RECEIVING: **LSU** — Michael Clayton 9-83; Devery Henderson 3-74; Skyler Green 2-20. **Ole Miss** — Chris Collins 3-39; Bill Flowers 2-74

INDIVIDUAL DEFENSIVE STATISTICS

INTERCEPTIONS: **LSU** — Corey Webster 1-0. **Ole Miss** — Jayme Mitchell 1-0; Von Hutchins 1-3; Travis Johnson 1-6

SACKS (unassisted-assisted): **LSU** — Marquise Hill 1-0; Kyle Williams 1-0; Melvin Oliver 1-0. **Ole Miss** — Josh Cooper 1-1; Daniel Booth 1-0; T. Blanchard 0-1

TACKLES (unassisted-assisted): **LSU** — LaRon Landry 6-2; Cameron Vaughn 4-3; Eric Alexander 4-1; Lionel Turner 3-2; Jack Hunt 2-3; Chad Lavalais 1-4; Corey Webster 3-0; Bennie Brazell 3-0; Marcus Spears 2-1. **Ole Miss** — L.P. Spence 4-5; Justin Wade 5-3

TIGERS' UNYIELDING DEFENSE PUTS A HEX ON MANNING MAGIC

BY PETER FINNEY
COLUMNIST

More than anything, this one was a throwback to the '50s, when the LSU Tigers were winning with a lot more than the offensive heroics of All-American Billy Cannon.

In those days, it was D-fence, D-fence, D-fence, with trench warfare in full fashion, with LSU and Ole Miss waging mini-score battles like 7-3, 6-6, 10-7.

And so it was in this classic 17-14 victory at Vaught-Hemingway Stadium as Nick Saban's third-ranked football team climbed to 10-1, keeping its championship hopes alive — SEC championship and national championship — in a game of violent defensive chess against the finest college quarterback in the country.

"They play the kind of defense that gives you a chance to make big plays," a harassed Eli Manning said. "But making them sure isn't easy."

On this afternoon, with the sun long gone, the last of the Mannings made a few big plays. But he didn't make near enough in a game when the winning quarterback, Matt Mauck, was giving up a quick score with the first of his three interceptions and managing to keep the door open for Eli to work his magic.

Eli Manning, who later finished third in the Heisman Trophy balloting, feels the heat as LSU defensive end Marcus Spears applies pressure in the fourth quarter.

STAFF PHOTO
BY ALEX BRANDON

STAFF PHOTO BY ALEX BRANDON

With the game on the line late in the fourth quarter, quarterback Eli Manning and the Rebels' chances fall by the wayside after a strong Tigers push up the middle causes him to stumble on a fourth-down play.

Just when all seemed lost for the home team, Manning found some of that magic dust, moving his team 76 yards on nine plays, converting three clutch third-down situations to pull the Rebels within field-goal range with just under 11 minutes remaining.

Yes, the war was on.

On the next Ole Miss series, back came Manning and the Rebels again, this time moving 68 yards, to the LSU 18, from which place-kicker Jonathan Nichols sent a 36-yard attempt wide right.

It wasn't over.

LSU went three-and-out. And there was Manning, having found his touch, with 1:50 left, camped on his 32-yard-line, with enough time to put his team in position for another crack at sending it into overtime.

"It was a time when the defense had to step way, way up," Saban said. "I just loved the way they handled that last series."

On first down, Manning was forced into a hurried incompletion.

On second down, he fired one down the middle, into the arms of Mike Espy at the LSU 40, but only for a second, when Jack Hunt delivered a monster hit to separate Espy from the football and force the incompletion.

On third down, Manning went over the middle again, only to watch a fast-closing Corey Webster get both hands on the ball, then drop it.

On fourth down, a hard-charging Chad Lavalais knocked back Ole Miss lineman Doug Buckles, creating a leg tangle that sent a retreating Manning down, for the final count.

"That hit by Jack Hunt was a monster play," Saban said. "If they complete it, they're all revved up, and who knows what might happen. Jack has been making big plays all season. You watch what he did out there, and you realize we really missed him when he didn't play against Florida."

You watched the LSU defense, and you realized what Eli Manning, hard-pressed to connect on 16 of 36 passes, was up against.

Tigers quarterback Matt Mauck, who threw three interceptions, including one on his first throw of the game that was returned by the Rebels for a touchdown, scrambles in the third quarter.

"They come after you, they're hard to push around, they're very talented, and they have the most extensive package of anyone we've played," Rebels offensive coordinator John Latina said. "We didn't execute well, and we had two weeks to prepare."

The Tigers did an outstanding job disguising their defensive fronts, their blitzes and their coverages.

"I give a lot of credit to Lionel Turner," Saban said of his linebacker who functioned as the defensive quarterback, calling what can best be described as defensive audibles. "It was Lionel's job to check out formations, to call coverages, to match wits, so to speak."

An Ole Miss offense that went into the game averaging 37 points had one touchdown. And an offense that was averaging 160 yards rushing finished with 27. And Manning, who was passing for 300 yards a game, ended with 200.

In the first half, when the Tigers' offensive woes were giving Manning prime field position, the Rebels wound up with three first downs and 79 yards in total offense, 11 on the ground.

"He was hard to rattle," Lavalais said of Manning, who was sacked three times. "But we did keep him off-balance. The big thing is we never stopped being aggressive. We kept taking it to them."

That was a high priority, given what Saban called a "tentative" performance on offense, mainly because LSU's line was getting whipped most of the time while his quarterback, except on rare instances, began to press.

"Matt has a tendency to press because he's so competitive," Saban said of someone who still found time to pass for two touchdowns. "Matt pressed, but he never got frustrated. That's the good thing. Now we move on."

Following a dismantling of Arkansas, LSU center Ben Wilkerson shows that the Tigers are tops in the SEC West.

STAFF PHOTO
BY ALEX BRANDON

GAME 12 | NOVEMBER 28, 2003

TIGER STADIUM | BATON ROUGE

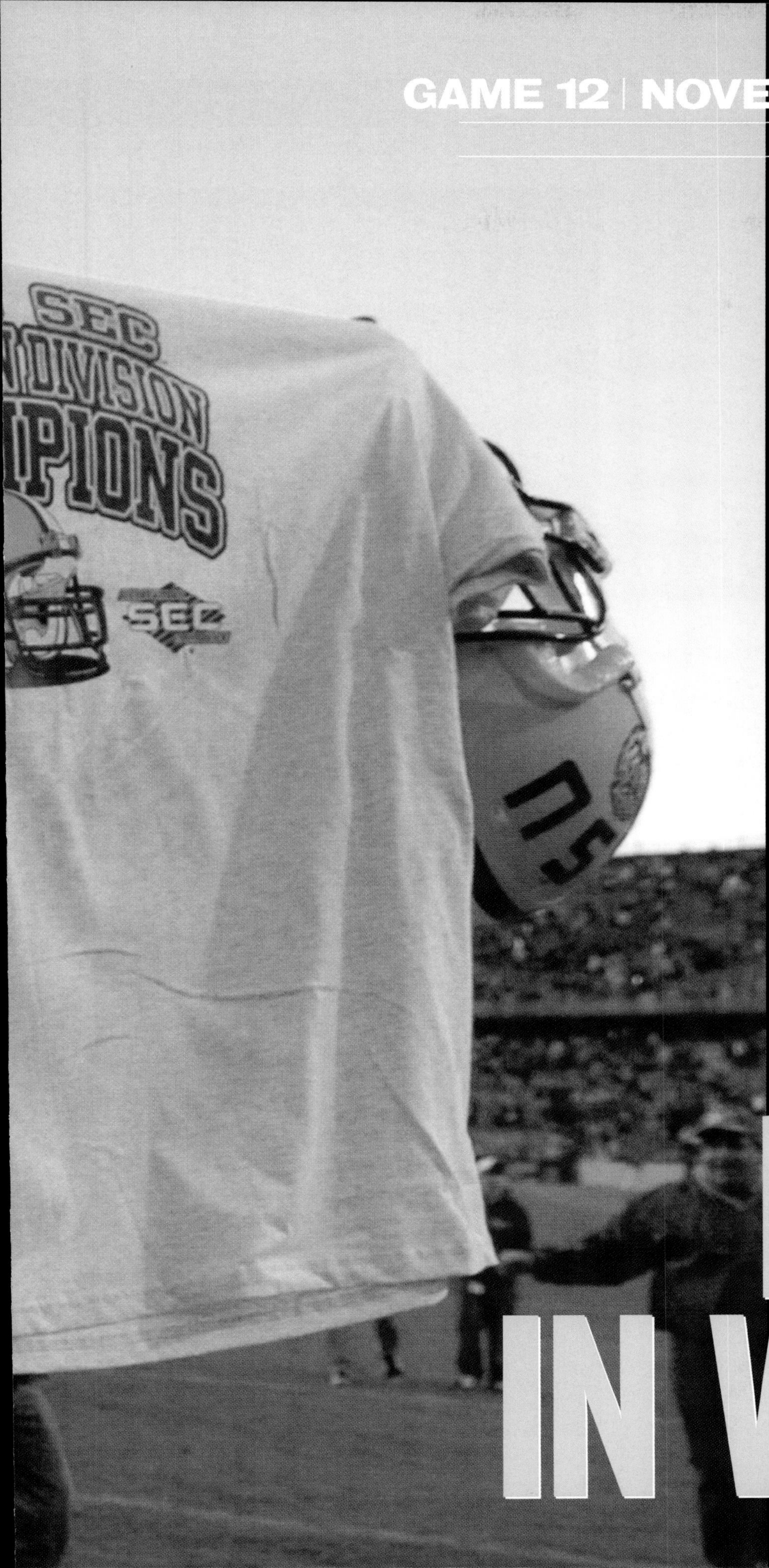

TIGERS WRAP UP DIVISION TITLE BY THRASHING RAZORBACKS

BEST IN WEST

LSU 55
ARKANSAS 24

LSU GOES TO SEC TITLE GAME WITH GEORGIA ON ITS MIND

BY MIKE TRIPLETT STAFF WRITER

LSU coach Nick Saban once said he was looking forward to a day when Tigers fans wouldn't rush the field after a big victory — as they did after beating Tennessee in 2000 and after clinching the SEC West against Auburn in 2001.

Saban wanted expectations to be higher in Baton Rouge. He wanted the next game to always be the most important one.

The coach got his wish in LSU's regular-season finale. The Tigers beat the Arkansas Razorbacks 55-24, clinching their second SEC West title in three years.

And the fans gave LSU a rousing approval — from their seats. These Tigers still have bigger Hogs to roast.

"Well, that's the way we want it to be," said Saban, who grabbed a microphone on the field after Friday's victory and thanked the fans. "Because next week, you get an even bigger challenge."

The win sent LSU to the SEC championship game in Atlanta to face the Georgia Bulldogs, co-champions of the SEC East.

LSU's mascot rides a wave of enthusiasm, just as the Tigers did after some initial resistance against the Razorbacks.

STAFF PHOTO BY CHUCK COOK

STAFF PHOTOS BY ALEX BRANDON

ABOVE, With LSU trailing 7-3 in the first quarter, defensive end Marcus Spears hits Arkansas quarterback Matt Jones, causing Jones to fumble the ball.

LEFT, The Tigers pounce on the opportunity as linebacker Eric Alexander scoops up the ball ...

As has been the case all year, LSU players took the Arkansas win in stride.

"You enjoy this for 24 hours," LSU receiver Michael Clayton said, referring to the team rule that says after 24 hours all focus turns toward the next game.

The Tigers already have accomplished more this season than any LSU team since the national championship squad in 1958.

They already have won 11 games for only the second time in school history. They won seven conference games for the first time in school history. And they have been ranked No. 3 in the nation for the past three weeks.

Perhaps most impressive, though, is how LSU has handled the role of front-runner in the SEC. The Tigers have won six straight games, with the pressure mounting each week.

"It's all about something Coach Saban told us two years ago when we were in this position," junior defensive end Marcus Spears said. " 'Only you can control your destiny.' And we knew that we had to win another game in order to go where we wanted to be."

The Razorbacks took an early 7-0 lead and tied the score at 17 in the second quarter, putting a brief scare into LSU.

After that, the Tigers scored 38 consecutive points to put the game out of reach.

"In the first quarter, both on offense and defense, we were a little jittery," said LSU quarterback Matt Mauck, who

... and with no one standing in his way, Alexander then races 25 yards for the score to lift LSU's spirits.

STAFF PHOTO BY ALEX BRANDON

STAFF PHOTO BY G. ANDREW BOYD

With the Razorbacks putting up a fight, wide receiver Michael Clayton, scoring on a 10-yard pass, and the Tigers pull out all the stops.

matched a career high with four touchdown passes. "I think it's just because we were excited to go out there and play. But by the second quarter, we really calmed down and were really playing well on both sides of the ball."

Arkansas entered the game with the SEC's No. 1-ranked rushing attack. LSU entered with the nation's No. 1-ranked rushing defense. Early in the game, the Razorbacks were winning the battle.

Arkansas tailback Cedric Cobbs gained 122 of his 169 yards in the first half — including runs of 61 and 20 yards on a two-play touchdown drive early in the second quarter.

But LSU's defense made up for its early woes by making big plays of its own. The Tigers forced five turnovers — including a fumble that was returned 25 yards for a touchdown by linebacker Eric Alexander in the first quarter, giving LSU a 10-7 lead.

LSU junior cornerback Corey Webster intercepted two passes, both of which set up touchdowns. It was sweet revenge for Webster, who last season allowed Arkansas to complete a 50-yard pass play in the final minute as the Razorbacks rallied to win 21-20.

Arkansas quarterback Matt Jones completed four of 12 passes for 100 yards, including a 53-yard screen pass to

ARKANSAS	10	7	0	7	24
LSU	10	24	21	0	55

SCORING SUMMARY

ARKANSAS Decori Birmingham 53-yard pass from Matt Jones (Chris Balseiro kick). Three plays, 61 yards in 1:11

LSU Chris Jackson 38-yard field goal. Eleven plays, 52 yards in 5:02

LSU Eric Alexander 25-yard fumble recovery (Jackson kick)

ARKANSAS Balseiro 40-yard field goal. Eight plays, 57 yards in 3:22

LSU Michael Clayton 10-yard pass from Matt Mauck (Jackson kick). Eight plays, 75 yards in 2:44

ARKANSAS Cedric Cobbs 20-yard run (Balseiro kick). Two plays, 76 yards in 22 seconds

LSU Skyler Green 2-yard pass from Mauck (Jackson kick). Three plays, 9 yards in 1:26

LSU Jackson 47-yard field goal. Nine plays, 38 yards in 3:50

LSU Devery Henderson 22-yard pass from Mauck (Jackson kick). Three plays, 36 yards in 25 seconds

LSU David Jones 37-yard pass from Mauck (Jackson kick). Two plays, 58 yards in 17 seconds

LSU Justin Vincent 23-yard run (Jackson kick). Eight plays, 57 yards in 5:13

LSU Vincent 2-yard run (Jackson kick). Six plays, 31 yards in 3:13

ARKANSAS Birmingham 16-yard pass from Jones (Balseiro kick). Ten plays, 80 yards in 4:45

TEAM STATISTICS

CATEGORY	ARKANSAS	LSU
FIRST DOWNS	14	24
RUSHES-YARDS (NET)	40-201	50-250
PASSING YARDS (NET)	100	186
PASSES ATT-COMP-INT	12-4-2	20-12-0
TOTAL OFFENSE PLAYS-YARDS	52-301	70-436
PUNT RETURNS-YARDS	2-14	2-25
KICKOFF RETURNS-YARDS	8-103	3-60
PUNTS (NUMBER-AVG)	4-43.0	3-39.3
FUMBLES-LOST	6-3	4-1
PENALTIES-YARDS	5-42	8-65
POSSESSION TIME	23:07	36:53
SACKS BY (NUMBER-YARDS)	0-0	0-0

INDIVIDUAL OFFENSIVE STATISTICS

RUSHING: **LSU** —Justin Vincent 18-112; Skyler Green 3-44; Matt Mauck 6-31; Joseph Addai 9-25; Barrington Edwards 9-14; Shyrone Carey 2-11. **Arkansas** — Cedric Cobbs 21-169

PASSING: **LSU** — Matt Mauck 12-19-0-186; Marcus Randall 0-1-0-0. **Arkansas** — Matt Jones 4-12-2-100

RECEIVING: **LSU** — Skyler Green 4-28; Michael Clayton 3-42; David Jones 2-57. **Arkansas** — Decori Birmingham 2-69

INDIVIDUAL DEFENSIVE STATISTICS

INTERCEPTIONS: **LSU** — Corey Webster 2-19. **Arkansas** — none

SACKS: **LSU** — Marcus Spears 1-0. **Arkansas** — none

TACKLES (unassisted-assisted): **LSU** — Jack Hunt 5-2; Eric Alexander 6-0; Jesse Daniels 5-1; Melvin Oliver 5-1; Chad White 5-1; Lionel Turner 3-3; Kyle Williams 2-4; Chad Lavalais 1-5. **Arkansas** — Caleb Miller 12-1; Tony Bua 9-3

Decori Birmingham for the game's first touchdown.

Eventually, LSU's offense started rolling. Tailback Justin Vincent rushed for 112 yards and two touchdowns, and the Tigers took a 55-17 lead in the third quarter.

"This is a team effort," said Mauck, who rebounded from one of the worst performances of his career in the previous week's 17-14 victory at Ole Miss. Mauck threw touchdown passes to Clayton, Devery Henderson, Skyler Green and David Jones.

"Our defense has played well all year long," Mauck said. "And they played well after the first quarter tonight. That's one thing we're always realizing, 'Hey, the defense has picked us up. Now it's our turn to help them out a little bit.'"

AP TOP 10		BCS RANKINGS	
RANK, SCHOOL	LAST WEEK	RANK, SCHOOL	TOTAL
1. OKLAHOMA	1	1. OKLAHOMA	2.06
2. SOUTHERN CAL	2	2. SOUTHERN CAL	6.90
3. LSU	3	3. LSU	8.43
4. MICHIGAN	4	4. MICHIGAN	10.22
5. GEORGIA	5	5. OHIO STATE	14.83
6. TEXAS	6	6. TEXAS	15.18
7. TENNESSEE	7	7. GEORGIA	15.33
8. OHIO STATE	8	8. FLORIDA STATE	18.44
9. FLORIDA STATE	9	9. TENNESSEE	20.37
10. MIAMI (FLA.)	10	10. MIAMI (FLA.)	20.89
Released Nov. 30		Released Dec. 1	

TIGERS WIN WEST WITH RISING CONFIDENCE

BY PETER FINNEY
COLUMNIST

Inside chilly Tiger Stadium, the roar was loud, the atmosphere was right out of Mardi Gras, and the signs were waving.

"ATLANTA HERE WE COME."

"SEE YOU IN THE DOME."

"BCS — THE WORLD IN CRISIS."

"CBS — Can't Beat Saban."

Euphoria reigned.

The answer to "How The West Was Won" was LSU 55, Arkansas 24.

Of course, there is still unfinished business.

Nick Saban's Tigers will head to the Georgia Dome for the regular-season finale and the chance to win their second SEC championship in three years.

But this time his team will be arriving in Atlanta under different circumstances. Two years ago they showed up as a three-times-beaten outsider, ranked 21st in the country, to play No. 2 Tennessee.

Two years later, the 11-1 Tigers will show up as the nation's No. 3 football team, with a chance to play for No. 1

Cornerback Corey Webster (13), flanked by cornerback Travis Daniels (29) and defensive tackle Chad Lavalais, is the center of attention after intercepting a pass in the third quarter.

STAFF PHOTO BY ALEX BRANDON

on Jan. 4 in the Nokia Sugar Bowl in New Orleans.

Two years ago the underdog Tigers pulled a 31-20 upset, knocked the Vols out of a shot at the national championship and finished the season ranked No. 8 after whipping Illinois in the Sugar Bowl.

Two years later the Tigers will play Georgia, co-champions of the SEC East, and the stakes keep rising.

Victory in Atlanta could mean a shot at the national championship — in New Orleans. Pinch yourself, Tiger fans.

"Let's just take time out to celebrate what we have," the winning coach said, his team having just tied coach Paul Dietzel's 1958 national championship Tigers for the most victories in a season by an LSU team, 11.

Saban talked like he was more happy than surprised. He had watched his team do again what it did the previous week against Ole Miss — start slowly, then come on to find a way to win. Last week it was defense that carried his Tigers. This time it was an offense that put the Razorbacks away with a 24-point second quarter. Quarterback Matt Mauck ended his afternoon with four touchdown passes and heavy applause from those close to him.

"You look at Matt," defensive end Marcus Spears said, "and you see a guy with confidence, the kind of confidence Coach Saban breeds in all of us. That's what coaching is all about, getting the right kind of players, having faith in them and getting them to play with confidence. That's what makes Coach Saban the coach he is. All you have to do is look at some of the young guys, guys like (freshman running back) Justin Vincent, like (freshman defensive back) Jessie Daniels who stepped up and made things happen. When it came to confidence, they were examples of the Saban touch."

LSU's confidence surfaced against an Arkansas team that came into Tiger Stadium on a four-game winning streak, a team that early in the season went into Austin and whipped Texas 38-28.

The Razorbacks made a statement in the first quarter, mainly with running back Cedric Cobbs, who rushed for 122 of his 169 yards in the first half.

By halftime, however, the LSU defense had slowed Cobbs and the offense came alive, breaking open a 17-17 game with a 17-0 salvo that finished with a 22-yard Mauck strike to Devery Henderson less than a minute before halftime.

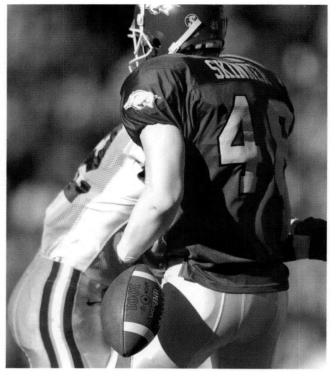

STAFF PHOTO BY ALEX BRANDON

Running back Barrington Edwards, who also plays on special teams, shows his worth by blocking the punt of Jacob Skinner in the second quarter.

"We kept going right at them," Henderson said. "We know we didn't play up to our standards last week. But we also know we've got guys who can make plays, just like the defense knows. We've grown into a team with great balance. We've just got to keep it going. Whoever we play in Atlanta will be a good team ready to knock us off."

Ask Saban for his memory of the Georgia Dome two years ago, and he'll recall "all that Tennessee orange" in the stands.

"The other thing I remember is gambling, going for it in the first half on fourth-and-inches inside our 25-yard line," he said. "We had fallen behind 14-7, and I was looking for a spark. When they stuffed us, I said to myself that had to be the dumbest call I ever made. I still feel that way."

After the game, Saban got a different slant on the gamble that was followed by Tennessee's missed field-goal attempt.

"Some players told me going for it showed the confidence I had in them," Saban said. "Honestly, I wasn't thinking about that when I made the call. What it shows you is you never know."

STAFF PHOTO BY ALEX BRANDON

Defensive tackle Melvin Oliver, right, and linebacker Cameron Vaughn make sure Arkansas quarterback Matt Jones isn't able to convert a third-and-short situation in the fourth quarter.

#25 JUSTIN VINCENT

L SU wasn't giving up on Justin Vincent as a tailback when it tried him out at defensive back for eight or nine practices in the spring of 2003. The coaches just wanted a contingency plan for their shallow secondary.

But the Tigers didn't know exactly what they had in the freshman.

Vincent took over LSU's starting tailback job six games into the season when the two players in front of him suffered injuries. He immediately ignited the Tigers and went over the 100-yard mark in four games.

But it was his performance in the SEC championship game that transfixed LSU fans. Vincent bolted for 201 yards and two touchdowns and was chosen the Most Valuable Player in LSU's dominating 34-13 victory over Georgia on Dec. 6 in Atlanta.

He also was named Most Outstanding Player in the Sugar Bowl, rushing for 117 yards and a touchdown.

"Well, coming in, I was able to get the position by two guys going down," Vincent said of junior Shyrone Carey and sophomore Joseph Addai. "I hate to see it go like that, but it's always an opportunity for somebody to step up."

Vincent knows something about missed opportunities. He was a high school standout and a Parade All-American, one of the centerpieces of LSU's 2002 recruiting class. But he failed to qualify academically by a fraction of a point.

Vincent voluntarily took some classes last fall to raise his grade-point average before enrolling at LSU in January. That's when he found himself in a crowded backfield with Carey and Addai, as well as two top freshmen recruits in Alley Broussard and Barrington Edwards.

"I just took it as it came," Vincent said.

LSU coach Nick Saban said Vincent is an example of what happens when you work hard and stay patient.

"We talk about it all the time," Saban said. "You work hard all the time to be able to take advantage of your opportunities. ... Everybody's heard that one, right? Well, this guy did that." — Mike Triplett

FULL NAME: Justin Daniel Vincent	FAMILY: Parents are Floyd and Lilly Vincent; brothers are Frank and Paul
BORN: Jan. 25, 1983	
BIRTHPLACE: Lake Charles	MAJOR: Mass communication
ATTENDED: Barbe High School	POSITION: Running back
	HEIGHT: 5 feet 10
	WEIGHT: 208 pounds

2003 HIGHLIGHTS

DATE	OPPONENT	CARRIES	YARDS	TDS
Oct. 25	Auburn	14	127	0
Nov. 22	Ole Miss	22	105	0
Nov. 28	Arkansas	18	112	2
Dec. 6	Georgia	18	201	2
Jan. 4	Oklahoma	16	117	1
Season totals		**154**	**1,001**	**10**

STAFF PHOTO BY ALEX BRANDON

LSU
34

GEORGIA
13

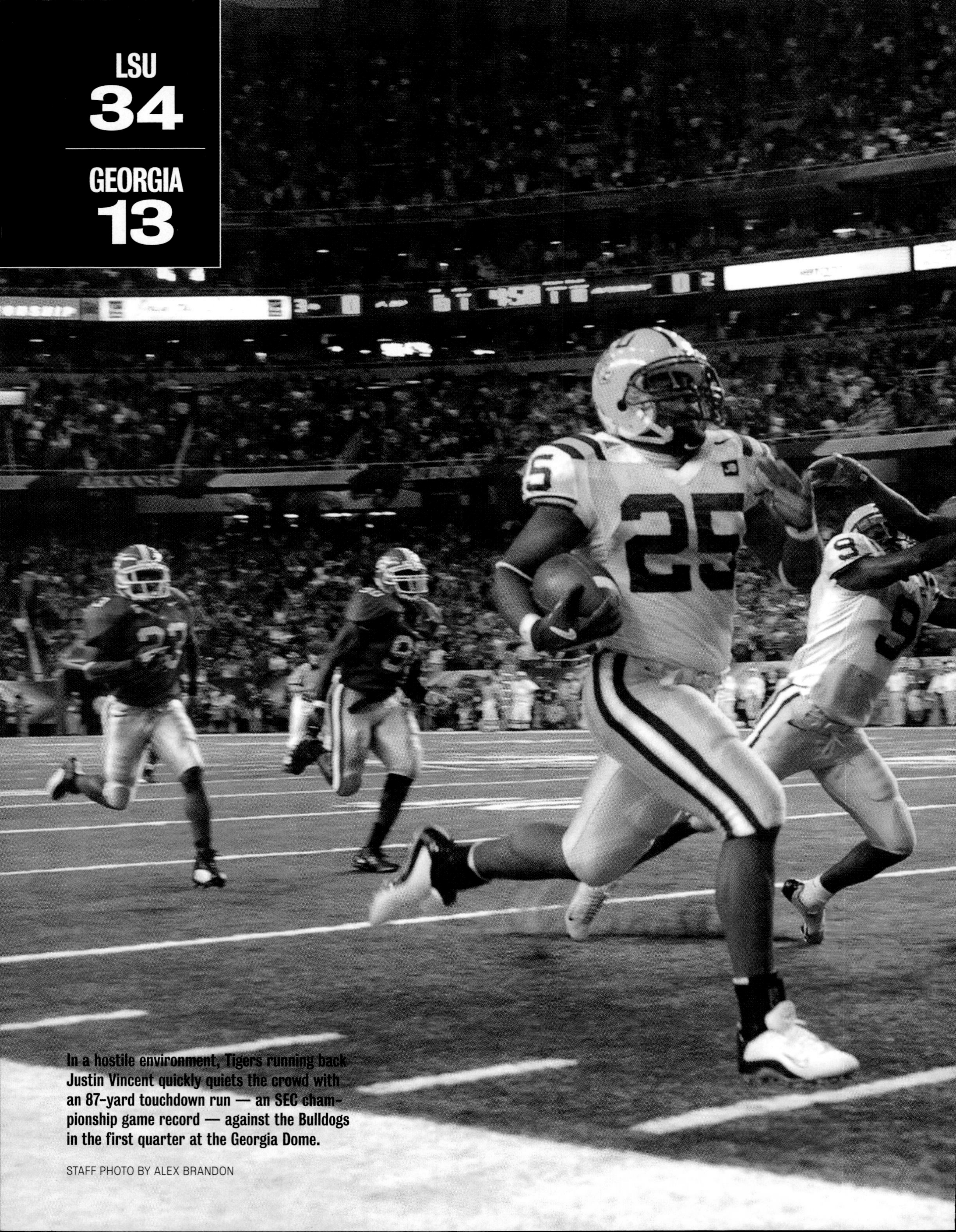

In a hostile environment, Tigers running back Justin Vincent quickly quiets the crowd with an 87-yard touchdown run — an SEC championship game record — against the Bulldogs in the first quarter at the Georgia Dome.

STAFF PHOTO BY ALEX BRANDON

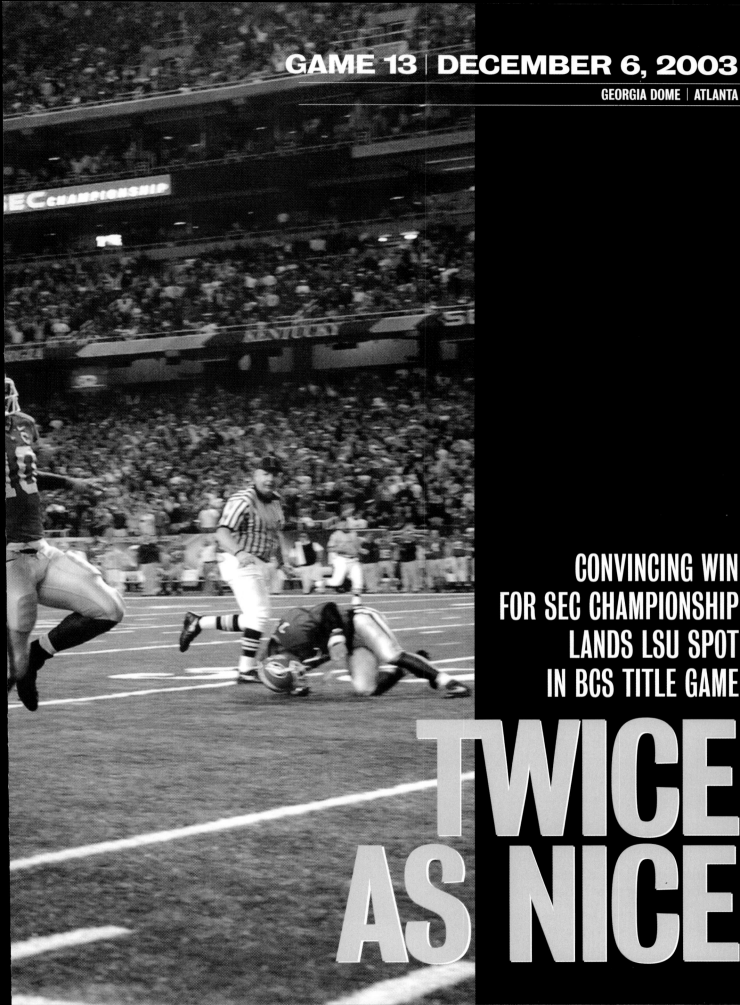

GAME 13 | DECEMBER 6, 2003

GEORGIA DOME | ATLANTA

CONVINCING WIN
FOR SEC CHAMPIONSHIP
LANDS LSU SPOT
IN BCS TITLE GAME

TWICE
AS NICE

LSU 34
GEORGIA 13

ONCE AGAIN, DEFENSE GETS THE JOB DONE FOR TIGERS

BY MIKE TRIPLETT STAFF WRITER

The LSU Tigers marched into Atlanta, and then ran over the Georgia Bulldogs.

The Tigers came home with a 34-13 victory in the SEC championship game, securing LSU's ninth conference title and first 12-win season in school history.

But it got even better: The dominating win over fifth-ranked Georgia catapulted LSU over Southern California and into second place in the crucial Bowl Championship Series rankings. After a steady climb all season by LSU, the pollsters and the computers agreed — the Tigers had earned the right to play Oklahoma in the Sugar Bowl for the BCS national championship.

On this night, though, that remained in the future. And LSU coach Nick Saban said it wasn't what the Tigers were playing for.

"I just want to say that I don't believe this team was motivated by what bowl game we would play in," Saban said. "They wanted to win the SEC. They wanted to prove to people that we were the best team in the league."

LSU keeps Georgia reeling as linebacker Lionel Turner returns an interception 18 yards for a touchdown in the third quarter.

STAFF PHOTO BY ALEX BRANDON

STAFF PHOTO BY ALEX BRANDON

LSU had six sacks against the Bulldogs, including defensive end Marcus Spears' takedown of David Greene on fourth down in the fourth quarter.

Wide receiver Michael Clayton, fending off defensive back Sean Jones in the first quarter, and the Tigers again had their way against the Bulldogs.

The SEC showdown was billed as a matchup between two of the top defenses in the country. But LSU's offense rose to the challenge early when freshman tailback Justin Vincent broke loose for an 87-yard touchdown run — the third-longest in school history — and quarterback Matt Mauck threw a 43-yard touchdown pass to receiver Michael Clayton.

Georgia tried to battle back, but the task proved insurmountable against a relentless LSU defense that lifted the Tigers all season.

The Tigers scored two of their points on a first-quarter safety and seven more when linebacker Lionel Turner returned an interception 18 yards for a touchdown in the third quarter.

"This is certainly one of the best groups that I've ever had the opportunity to be associated with," Saban said of an LSU defense that finished the season ranked No. 1 in the nation in fewest points allowed per game (10.8). "The chemistry is great, and it was something we were very concerned about

Punt returner Skyler Green fights for yardage against Greg Blue, helping the Tigers get good field position in the first quarter.

AP TOP 10

RANK, SCHOOL	LAST WEEK
1. SOUTHERN CAL	2
2. LSU	3
3. OKLAHOMA	1
4. MICHIGAN	4
5. TEXAS	6
6. TENNESSEE	7
7. OHIO STATE	8
8. KANSAS STATE	13
9. FLORIDA STATE	9
10. MIAMI (FLA.)	10

Released Dec. 7

BCS RANKINGS

RANK, SCHOOL	TOTAL
1. OKLAHOMA	5.11
2. LSU	5.99
3. SOUTHERN CAL	6.15
4. MICHIGAN	10.63
5. OHIO STATE	14.28
6. TEXAS	14.53
7. FLORIDA STATE	17.93
8. TENNESSEE	19.64
9. MIAMI (FLA.)	19.79
10. KANSAS STATE	22.73

Released Dec. 8

coming out of spring practice. It wasn't like anybody said we were going to have a dominant defense."

Mauck, who was the SEC championship game Most Valuable Player as a freshman two seasons ago, stepped up big once again. He completed 14 of 22 passes for 151 yards with a touchdown and an interception.

But he took a back seat to Vincent, who set an SEC championship game record with 201 rushing yards and two touchdowns.

Saban said Vincent made the 87-yard run happen practically on his own. And he said the Lake Charles native is a perfect example of what can come from hard work, patience and determination.

Before Saturday night's games kicked off, BCS analyst Jerry Palm already had said the Tigers would likely earn a spot in the Sugar Bowl with a victory because LSU's strength of schedule rating would improve enough to boost the Tigers into the second spot.

Palm turned out to be right, but Mauck said the team did not come into the game worried about it.

"All we could do is play the best game we could play against Georgia," Mauck said. "And hopefully somebody will take notice."

Georgia coach Mark Richt, however, said his mind was made up after his Bulldogs lost to the Tigers for the second time this season.

"They can beat anyone in the country," Richt said. "I'd feel a lot better about it if they won it all."

LSU	8	9	7	10	34
GEORGIA	0	3	10	0	13

SCORING SUMMARY

LSU Justin Vincent 87-yard run (Chris Jackson kick failed). One play, 87 yards in 19 seconds

LSU Team safety

LSU Michael Clayton 43-yard pass from Matt Mauck (Jackson kick failed). Seven plays, 71 yards in 3:20

LSU Ryan Gaudet 35-yard field goal. 8 plays, 20 yards in 3:27

GEORGIA Billy Bennett 51-yard field goal. 9 plays, 45 yards, 2:59

GEORGIA Bennett 49-yard field goal. Five plays, 12 yards in 1:22

LSU Lionel Turner 18-yard interception return (Gaudet kick)

GEORGIA Ben Watson 18-yard pass from David Greene (Bennett kick). Four plays, 72 yards in 37 seconds

LSU Vincent 3-yard run (Gaudet kick). Nine plays, 78 yards in 3:46

LSU Gaudet 22-yard field goal. Seven plays, 85 yards in 4:14

TEAM STATISTICS

CATEGORY	GEORGIA	LSU
FIRST DOWNS	14	17
RUSHES-YARDS (NET)	25-50	46-293
PASSING YARDS (NET)	199	151
PASSES ATT-COMP-INT	41-17-3	22-14-1
TOTAL OFFENSE PLAYS-YARDS	66-249	68-444
PUNT RETURNS-YARDS	3-1	3-33
KICKOFF RETURNS-YARDS	5-59	3-55
PUNTS (NUMBER-AVG)	6-38.7	6-42.7
FUMBLES-LOST	0-0	1-0
PENALTIES-YARDS	3-24	5-45
POSSESSION TIME	24:22	35:38
SACKS BY (NUMBER-YARDS)	4-35	6-53

INDIVIDUAL OFFENSIVE STATISTICS

RUSHING: **LSU** — Justin Vincent 18-201; Joseph Addai 8-60; Alley Broussard 11-47. **Georgia** — Kregg Lumpkin 7-54; Reggie Brown 1-35; David Greene 5 minus-49

PASSING: **LSU** — Matt Mauck 14-22-1-151. **Georgia** — David Greene 17-41-3-199

RECEIVING: **LSU** — Michael Clayton 5-81; Devery Henderson 4-47; Skyler Green 3-11. **Georgia** — Ben Watson 4-86; Fred Gibson 3-19

INDIVIDUAL DEFENSIVE STATISTICS

INTERCEPTIONS: **LSU** — Jack Hunt 1-0; Lionel Turner 1-18; LaRon Landry 1-0. **Georgia** — Bruce Thornton 1-0

SACKS (unassisted-assisted): **LSU** — Eric Alexander 1-1; Corey Webster 0-1; Randall Gay 1-0; Marquise Hill 1-0; Chad Lavalais 1-0; Marcus Spears 1-0. **Georgia** — Odell Thurman 1-0; Robert Geathers 1-0; David Pollack 1-0; Sean Jones 1-0

TACKLES (unassisted-assisted): **LSU** — Travis Daniels 5-1; LaRon Landry 4-1; Jack Hunt 3-2; Eric Alexander 3-3; Chad Lavalais 3-0; Randall Gay 3-1; Lionel Turner 1-5. **Georgia** — Thomas Davis 5-6; Odell Thurman 4-7; Greg Blue 4-5

TIGERS' JOY RIDE ON FAST TRACK TO SUGAR BOWL

BY PETER FINNEY
COLUMNIST

Hello, New Orleans. The LSU Tigers are coming home.

And no matter what happens in the Superdome on Jan. 4, bank on the guys in the yellow hats to put on a show.

There's a kind of epic poetry to the LSU Tigers, who buried the Georgia Bulldogs 34-13 in the SEC championship game and will play Oklahoma in the Bowl Championship Series championship game.

I'm writing this just as Marcus Spears is roaring in to bury David Greene, the Georgia quarterback, on the Bulldogs' final chance to score a second touchdown.

I'm writing this long after many of the red-shirted Bulldog fans have taken almost all of the red out of the Georgia Dome.

The true beauty of this bunch of Tigers reflects the hand of the head coach, Nick Saban, and the speedy group of blitzers he has brought into Tigertown.

Deservedly, Justin Vincent, who ran for 201 yards and two touchdowns, rushed away with the Most Valuable Player tro-

Following the dismantling of the Bulldogs, offensive guard Terrell McGill celebrates the Tigers' second SEC championship in three seasons.

STAFF PHOTO BY MATT ROSE

phy. But make no mistake. LSU is a football team that wins with defense, with toughness and quickness up front, to go along with blazing speed behind it.

When it comes to a team MVP, the vote usually leans to Chad Lavalais, whose long arms have made life miserable for opposing quarterbacks. But this is a defense that goes far beyond the whirling dervish tackle. You try to paint the picture, and you think of a number of things. LaRon Landry slicing up the middle. Jack Hunt beginning his run 10 yards behind the line and winding up in the lap of the quarterback. Lionel Turner jamming the passing lane and picking one off for six points.

You remember these things, and you're not surprised David Greene struggled mightily to complete 17 of his 41 throws, three of them to the other team.

You remember the way Lavalais, Spears and his two other henchmen in the trenches, Marquis Hill and Kyle Williams, threw their weight around and you know why Georgia, limited to 50 rushing yards on 25 carries, gave up on the ground and kept putting it in the air, hoping for happy landings.

The manner in which LSU's defense dominated, the way it never allowed the Bulldogs to approach any kind of rhythm, made it no surprise Georgia's only touchdown of the evening was set up by a 35-yard run (and a 15-yard facemask penalty) after a left-end sweep turned into a right-end sweep.

It was that kind of frustrating night for the losers.

As for the winners, and the architect, it was wall-to-wall satisfaction.

"All I can say is this is the most fun year I've ever had as a coach," Saban said. "It comes down to the older players setting a great example for the younger ones."

On this evening, LSU began sending a message, early and often, from all angles.

In the first quarter, you could not blame Greene for feeling it was still September and he was back in Tiger Stadium. Saban's blitzes were coming up the middle and off the corners. They were being timed perfectly, forcing the Georgia quarterback to rush some of his throws, to hesitate just enough to misfire.

After the Dawgs returned a blocked field-goal attempt to

STAFF PHOTO BY ALEX BRANDON

Winning never gets old, but safety Jack Hunt and LSU fans especially relish beating the Bulldogs at the Georgia Dome.

the Tigers' 31, LSU faked a blitz and a Greene pass down the gut was picked off by Landry. It was Greene's first interception in 110 attempts.

Moments later, with the Tigers playing a first down at their 13, Vincent took a pitch from Mauck and shot up the right side for 87 yards, the longest scamper in an SEC championship game, finding daylight behind a key block by Ben Wilkerson, then two more downfield by tight end Davey Jones and wideout Devery Henderson.

"Justin made that run mostly on his own," Saban said. "I think it was probably the biggest play of the game."

Moments later, a jittery punter handed LSU a safety when he couldn't handle the snap. It all happened in the first 15 minutes, a span that found two freshmen, Vincent and Alley Broussard, and sophomore Joseph Addai, rushing for 128 yards.

By the time Mauck hit Michael Clayton down the middle to make it a 14-0 ballgame, the Tigers were averaging 10 yards a play, the Bulldogs a meager 0.1.

Meanwhile, Saban was sticking with the blitz, nailing Greene for a minus-33 yards and limiting the Dawgs to a minus-18 yards on 13 first-half rushes.

For Georgia, it never ended.

For LSU, the fun is only beginning.

Coach Nick Saban and the Tigers, the 2003 SEC champions, finished the regular season 12-1, earning the most wins in school history.

LSU TEAM STATISTICS AS OF DEC. 8, 2003

CATEGORY	LSU	OPP.
SCORING	454	140
POINTS PER GAME	34.92	10.8
FIRST DOWNS	285	179
RUSHING	133	67
PASSING	135	94
PENALTY	17	18
RUSHING YARDAGE	2,441	886
YARDS GAINED RUSHING	2,799	1,465
YARDS LOST RUSHING	358	579
RUSHING ATTEMPTS	553	367
AVERAGE PER RUSH	4.4	2.4
AVERAGE PER GAME	187.8	68.2
TOUCHDOWNS RUSHING	22	3
PASSING YARDAGE	3,104	2,488
ATT-COMP-INT	377-241-13	440-200-19
AVERAGE PER PASS	8.2	5.7
AVERAGE PER CATCH	12.9	12.4

	LSU	OPP.
AVERAGE PER GAME	238.8	191.4
TOUCHDOWNS PASSING	30	12
TOTAL OFFENSE	5,545	3,374
TOTAL PLAYS	930	807
AVERAGE PER PLAY	6.0	4.2
AVERAGE PER GAME	426.5	259.5
KICK RETURNS (NUMBER-YDS)	23-514	57-954
PUNT RETURNS (NUMBER-YDS)	43-641	26-148
INT RETURNS (NUMBER-YARDS)	19-200	13-104
KICK RETURN AVERAGE	22.3	16.7
PUNT RETURN AVERAGE	14.9	5.7
INT RETURN AVERAGE	10.5	8.0
FUMBLES-LOST	25-12	21-12
PENALTIES-YARDS	94-780	87-606
AVERAGE PER GAME	60.0	46.6
PUNTS-YARDS	58-2,485	94-3,767
AVERAGE PER PUNT	42.8	40.1
NET PUNT AVERAGE	40.3	33.3

TIME OF POSSESSION (GAME)	33:37	26:23
THIRD-DOWN CONVERSIONS	77/181	45/189
THIRD-DOWN PERCENTAGE	43	24
FOURTH-DOWN CONVERSIONS	10/18	8/23
FOURTH-DOWN PERCENTAGE	56	35
SACKS BY-YARDS	39-320	17-136
MISCELLANEOUS YARDS	40	33
TOUCHDOWNS SCORED	60	17
FIELD GOALS-ATTEMPTS	12-20	8-17
EXTRA POINT ATTEMPTS	54-58	14-15
ATTENDANCE (AVERAGE)	8/88,966	564,168

SCORE BY QUARTERS

TEAM	1ST	2ND	3RD	4TH	TOTAL
LSU	123	154	108	69	454
OPPONENTS	30	16	37	57	140

INDIVIDUAL OFFENSIVE STATISTICS AS OF DEC. 8, 2003

RUSHING

Player	GP	Att	Gain	Loss	Net	Avg	TD	Long	Avg/G
Justin Vincent	13	138	905	21	884	6.4	9	87	68.0
Joseph Addai	11	112	545	24	521	4.7	2	21	47.4
Alley Broussard	11	83	402	19	383	4.6	4	33	34.8
Shyrone Carey	8	78	366	28	338	4.3	6	35	42.2
Barrington Edwards	11	41	191	22	169	4.1	0	32	15.4
Matt Mauck	13	65	213	143	70	1.1	1	16	5.4
Skyler Green	13	5	71	3	68	13.6	0	17	5.2
Devery Henderson	13	8	39	2	37	4.6	0	13	2.8
Michael Clayton	13	3	25	0	25	8.3	0	17	1.9
Marcus Randall	8	9	40	25	15	1.7	0	15	1.9
Blain Bech	6	1	2	0	2	2.0	0	2	0.3
Team	7	10	0	71	-71	-7.1	0	0	-10.1
Total	13	553	2,799	358	2,441	4.4	22	87	187.8
Opponents	13	367	1,465	579	886	2.4	3	62	68.2

PASSING

Player	GP	Effic	Att-Cmp-Int	Pct	Yds	TD	Lng	Avg/G
Matt Mauck	13	152.17	336-216-12	64.3	2,701	28	64	207.8
Marcus Randall	8	158.63	40-25-1	62.5	403	2	66	50.4
Michael Clayton	13	0.00	1-0-0	0.0	0	0	0	0.0
Total	13	152.45	377-241-13	63.9	3,104	30	66	238.8
Opponents	13	93.32	440-200-19	45.5	2,488	12	93	191.4

RECEIVING

Player	GP	No.	Yds	Avg	TD	Long	Avg/G
Michael Clayton	13	74	1,041	14.1	10	66	80.1
Devery Henderson	13	51	837	16.4	11	64	64.4
Skyler Green	13	46	496	10.8	5	40	38.2
Eric Edwards	13	15	153	10.2	2	23	11.8
Joseph Addai	11	12	74	6.2	1	25	6.7
David Jones	11	10	178	17.8	1	37	16.2
Dwayne Bowe	9	9	106	11.8	0	24	11.8
Justin Vincent	13	8	80	10.0	0	19	6.2
Craig Davis	7	7	63	9.0	0	17	9.0
Keith Zinger	8	3	31	10.3	0	15	3.9
Demetri Robinson	8	2	24	12.0	0	15	3.0
Shyrone Carey	8	1	10	10.0	0	10	1.2
Gino Giambelluca	10	1	5	5.0	0	5	0.5
Alley Broussard	11	1	5	5.0	0	5	0.5
Barrington Edwards	11	1	1	1.0	0	1	0.1
Total	13	241	3,104	12.9	30	66	238.8
Opponents	13	200	2,488	12.4	12	93	191.4

PUNT RETURNS

Player	No.	Yds	Avg	TD	Long
Skyler Green	22	436	19.8	2	80
Shyrone Carey	18	195	10.8	0	35
Travis Daniels	2	10	5.0	0	0
Ronnie Prude	1	0	0.0	0	0
Total	43	641	14.9	2	80
Opponents	26	148	5.7	0	23

INTERCEPTIONS

Player	No.	Yds	Avg	TD	Long
Corey Webster	6	42	7.0	0	16
Jack Hunt	4	94	23.5	2	34
LaRon Landry	2	0	0.0	0	0
Lionel Turner	2	21	10.5	1	18
Travis Daniels	2	48	24.0	1	48
Chad Lavalais	1	-5	-5.0	0	0
Ronnie Prude	1	0	0.0	0	0
Kyle Williams	1	0	0.0	0	0
Total	19	200	10.5	4	48
Opponents	13	104	8.0	1	44

KICK RETURNS

Player	No.	Yds	Avg	TD	Long
Devery Henderson	13	286	22.0	0	48
Skyler Green	9	188	20.9	0	32
Bennie Brazell	1	40	40.0	0	40
Total	23	514	22.3	0	48
Opponents	57	954	16.7	0	42

FUMBLE RETURNS

Player	No.	Yds	Avg	TD	Long
Eric Alexander	1	25	25.0	1	25
Jason LeDoux	1	15	15.0	1	15
Total	2	40	20.0	2	25
Opponents	3	33	11.0	1	29

SCORING

Player	TD	FGs	Kick	Rush	Rcv	Pass	DXP	Saf	Points
Devery Henderson	11	0-0	0-0	0-0	0	0-0	0	0	66
Michael Clayton	10	0-0	0-0	0-0	0	0-0	0	0	60
Ryan Gaudet	0	7-12	33-35	0-0	0	0-0	0	0	54
Justin Vincent	9	0-0	0-0	0-0	0	0-0	0	0	54
Skyler Green	7	0-0	0-0	0-0	0	0-0	0	0	42
Shyrone Carey	6	0-0	0-0	0-0	0	0-0	0	0	36

Player	TD	FG	PAT	Rush		Rec			Pts
Chris Jackson	0	5-8	21-23	0-0	0	0-0	0	0	36
Alley Broussard	4	0-0	0-0	0-0	0	0-0	0	0	24
Joseph Addai	3	0-0	0-0	0-0	0	0-0	0	0	18
Eric Edwards	2	0-0	0-0	0-0	0	0-0	0	0	12
Jack Hunt	2	0-0	0-0	0-0	0	0-0	0	0	12
Matt Mauck	1	0-0	0-0	1-2	0	0-0	0	0	8
David Jones	1	0-0	0-0	0-0	0	0-0	0	0	6
Travis Daniels	1	0-0	0-0	0-0	0	0-0	0	0	6
Lionel Turner	1	0-0	0-0	0-0	0	0-0	0	0	6
Jason LeDoux	1	0-0	0-0	0-0	0	0-0	0	0	6
Eric Alexander	1	0-0	0-0	0-0	0	0-0	0	0	6
Team	0	0-0	0-0	0-0	0	0-0	0	1	2
Total	60	12-20	54-58	1-2	0	0-0	0	1	454
Opponents	17	8-17	14-15	0-0	0	0-2	0	0	140

TOTAL OFFENSE

Player	G	Plays	Rush	Pass	Total	Avg/G
Matt Mauck	13	401	70	2,701	2,771	213.2
Justin Vincent	13	138	884	0	884	68.0
Joseph Addai	11	112	521	0	521	47.4
Marcus Randall	8	49	15	403	418	52.2
Alley Broussard	11	83	383	0	383	34.8
Shyrone Carey	8	78	338	0	338	42.2
Barrington Edwards	11	41	169	0	169	15.4
Skyler Green	13	5	68	0	68	5.2
Devery Henderson	13	8	37	0	37	2.8
Michael Clayton	13	4	25	0	25	1.9
Blain Bech	6	1	2	0	2	0.3
Team	7	10	-71	0	-71	-10.1
Total	13	930	2,441	3,104	5,545	426.5
Opponents	13	807	886	2,488	3,374	259.5

FIELD GOALS

Player	FGM-FGA	Pct	01-19	20-29	30-39	40-49	50-99	Lg	Blk
Ryan Gaudet	7-12	58.3	0-0	1-1	4-6	2-4	0-1	47	2
Chris Jackson	5-8	62.5	0-0	1-1	2-3	2-4	0-0	47	1

PUNTING

Player	No.	Yds	Avg	Long	TB	FC	I20	Blk
Donnie Jones	58	2,485	42.8	67	7	14	21	0
Total	58	2,485	42.8	67	7	14	21	0
Opponents	94	3,767	40.1	66	7	11	16	2

ALL PURPOSE

Player	G	Rush	Rec	PR	KOR	IR	Tot	Avg/G
Skyler Green	13	68	496	436	188	0	1,188	91.4
Devery Henderson	13	37	837	0	286	0	1,160	89.2
Michael Clayton	13	25	1,041	0	0	0	1,066	82.0
Justin Vincent	13	884	80	0	0	0	964	74.2
Joseph Addai	11	521	74	0	0	0	595	54.1
Shyrone Carey	8	338	10	195	0	0	543	67.9
Alley Broussard	11	383	5	0	0	0	388	35.3
David Jones	11	0	178	0	0	0	178	16.2
Barrington Edwards	11	169	1	0	0	0	170	15.5
Eric Edwards	13	0	153	0	0	0	153	11.8
Dwayne Bowe	9	0	106	0	0	0	106	11.8
Jack Hunt	12	0	0	0	0	94	94	7.8
Matt Mauck	13	70	0	0	0	0	70	5.4
Craig Davis	7	0	63	0	0	0	63	9.0
Travis Daniels	13	0	0	10	0	48	58	4.5
Corey Webster	13	0	0	0	0	42	42	3.2
Bennie Brazell	9	0	0	0	40	0	40	4.4
Keith Zinger	8	0	31	0	0	0	31	3.9
Demetri Robinson	8	0	24	0	0	0	24	3.0
Lionel Turner	13	0	0	0	0	21	21	1.6
Marcus Randall	8	15	0	0	0	0	15	1.9
Gino Giambelluca	10	0	5	0	0	0	5	0.5
Blain Bech	6	2	0	0	0	0	2	0.3
Chad Lavalais	13	0	0	0	0	-5	-5	-0.4
Team	7	-71	0	0	0	0	-71	-10.1
Total	13	2,441	3,104	641	514	200	6,900	530.8
Opponents	13	886	2,488	148	954	104	4,580	352.3

INDIVIDUAL DEFENSIVE STATISTICS AS OF DEC. 8, 2003

Player	GP	Solo	Ast	Tot.	TFL-Yds	No-Yds	Int-Yds	BrUp	Rcv-Yds	FF	Kick	Saf
LaRon Landry	13	53	23	76	3.5-31	3-30	2-0	4	-	-	1	-
Lionel Turner	13	42	27	69	3.0-14	1-11	2-21	5	-	2	-	-
Jack Hunt	12	44	23	67	3.0-4	-	4-94	6	-	-	-	-
Eric Alexander	13	46	11	57	8.0-33	5-36	-	5	2-25	1	-	-
Chad Lavalais	13	30	27	57	16.0-85	7-52	1-5	6	-	-	1	-
Travis Daniels	13	41	13	54	5.5-35	2-22	2-48	25	1-0	-	1	-
Cameron Vaughn	13	27	26	53	3.0-14	2-12	-	3	1-0	-	-	-
Marcus Spears	13	30	17	47	12.0-69	5-47	-	6	1-0	2	-	-
Corey Webster	13	36	10	46	3.5-13	1-5	6-42	23	-	1	-	-
Kyle Williams	13	17	21	38	6.5-45	4-37	1-0	-	-	-	-	-
Marquise Hill	12	19	17	36	9.5-40	5-26	-	1	-	-	-	-
Jesse Daniels	12	22	10	32	1.0-4	-	-	4	-	-	-	-
Randall Gay	11	22	8	30	4.0-29	2-25	-	11	-	-	-	-
Bryce Wyatt	13	12	16	28	2.5-4	-	-	4	-	-	-	-
Melvin Oliver	12	13	14	27	2.0-13	3-13	-	2	2-0	-	-	-
Ronnie Prude	12	14	9	23	-	-	1-0	8	-	-	-	-
Kirston Pittman	12	6	9	15	2.0-14	2-25	-	1	1-0	1	-	-
Jason LeDoux	10	7	8	15	-	-	-	1	1-15	-	-	-
Daniel Francis	11	9	6	15	0.5-7	-	-	1	1-0	-	-	-
Michael Clayton	13	14	-	14	-	-	-	-	-	-	-	-
Adrian Mayes	11	6	7	13	1.0-5	-	-	1	1-0	1	-	-
Chad White	10	9	2	11	-	-	-	-	1-0	-	-	-
Brian West	6	6	4	10	4.5-17	2-9	-	1	-	-	-	-
Gino Giambelluca	10	4	6	10	-	-	-	-	-	-	1	-
Brandon Washington	10	5	5	10	-	-	-	-	-	-	1	-
Justin Vincent	13	5	4	9	-	-	-	-	-	-	-	-
Bennie Brazell	9	4	3	7	-	-	-	-	-	-	-	-
Dave Peterson	7	5	1	6	2.5-7	1-0	-	-	-	1	-	-
Steve Damen	11	3	3	6	-	-	-	-	-	-	-	-
Barrington Edwards	11	2	3	5	-	-	-	-	-	-	-	-
Chris Jackson	13	5	-	5	-	-	-	-	-	-	-	-
Torran Williams	7	1	4	5	1.0-3	-	-	-	-	-	-	-
Philip Maxwell	4	3	1	4	-	-	-	-	-	-	-	-
Keron Gordon	5	2	1	3	-	-	-	-	-	-	-	-
Ryan Willis	3	1	1	2	-	-	-	-	-	-	-	-
Alley Broussard	11	1	1	2	0.5-8	-	-	-	-	-	-	-
Joseph Addai	11	2	-	2	-	-	-	-	-	-	-	-
Devery Henderson	13	2	-	2	-	-	-	-	-	-	-	-
Matt Mauck	13	1	-	1	-	-	-	-	-	-	-	-
Stephen Peterman	10	1	-	1	-	-	-	-	-	-	-	-
Jarvus Ryes	2	-	1	1	0.5-0	-	-	-	-	1	-	-
Nick Child	4	1	-	1	-	-	-	-	-	-	-	-
Dorestt Buckels	2	-	1	1	-	-	-	-	-	-	-	-
Rodney Reed	9	1	-	1	-	-	-	-	-	-	-	-
Willie Demps	3	1	-	1	1.0-2	-	-	-	-	1	-	-
Donnie Jones	13	1	-	1	-	-	-	-	-	-	-	-
Marcus Randall	8	1	-	1	-	-	-	-	-	-	-	-
Team	7	-	-	-	-	-	-	-	-	-	-	1
Total	13	577	343	920	96-496	39-320	19-200	120	12-40	11	3	1
Opponents	13	-	-	-	-	17-136	13-104	33	12-33	12	4	-

2003 LSU ROSTER

Number, name	Pos.	Hgt	Wgt	Yr.	Hometown	H.S. or college
1 Ronnie Prude	CB	5-11	176	Jr.	Shreveport	Fair Park
1 Amp Hill	WR	6-3	203	Fr.	Jacksonville, Fla.	First Coast
2 Shyrone Carey	RB	5-6	198	Jr.	New Orleans	Shaw
4 JaMarcus Russell	QB	6-5	236	Fr.	Mobile, Ala.	Williamson
5 Skyler Green	WR	5-9	190	So.	Westwego	Higgins
7 Adrian Mayes	LB	6-1	213	Sr.	Houston	Forest Brook
8 Jack Hunt	FS	6-1	197	Sr.	Ruston	Ruston
8 Terrell Clayton	WR	5-9	158	Fr.	Shreveport	Byrd
9 Devery Henderson	WR	6-0	189	Sr.	Opelousas	Opelousas
10 Joseph Addai	RB	6-0	205	So.	Houston	Sharpstown
12 Marcus Randall	QB	6-2	223	Jr.	Baton Rouge	Glen Oaks
13 Corey Webster	CB	6-0	201	Jr	Vacherie	St. James
13 Steve Mares	WR	5-7	165	Jr.	Santa Rosa, Calif.	Santa Rosa J.C.
14 Michael Clayton	WR	6-4	200	Jr.	Baton Rouge	Christian Life
15 Matt Flynn	QB	6-2	224	Fr.	Tyler, Texas	Lee
17 Bennie Brazell	WR	6-1	166	So.	Houston	Westbury
18 Matt Mauck	QB	6-2	213	Jr.	Jasper, Ind.	Jasper
19 Darius Ingram	LB	6-2	232	Fr.	Tenaha, Texas	Tenaha
21 Randall Gay	CB	5-11	178	Sr.	Brusly	Brusly
22 Alley Broussard	RB	6-0	235	Fr.	Lafayette	Acadiana
24 Keron Gordon	CB	6-1	188	Fr.	Tampa, Fla.	Plant
25 Justin Vincent	RB	5-10	208	Fr.	Lake Charles	Barbe
26 Nick Child	DB	6-0	169	Fr.	Metairie	Rummel
27 Eric Alexander	LB	6-3	223	Sr.	Port Arthur, Texas	Austin
28 Greg Hercules	SS	6-1	195	Jr.	Palatine, Ill.	Palatine
29 Travis Daniels	FS	6-1	187	Jr.	Hollywood, Fla.	South Broward
30 LaRon Landry	DB	6-2	180	Fr.	Boutte	Hanhville
31 Jessie Daniels	DB	5-11	195	Fr.	Breaux Bridge	Breaux Bridge
32 Barrington Edwards	RB	6-0	213	Fr.	Bowie, Md.	Bowie
33 Jonathan Zenon	DB	6-0	172	Fr.	Breaux Bridge	Breaux Bridge
34 Dorsett Buckels	LB	5-11	221	Jr.	Amite	Amite
35 Brandon Nowlin	FB	5-10	220	Sr.	Baton Rouge	Catholic
36 Patrick Fisher	P	6-5	224	Fr.	Hyattsville, Md.	DeMatha
37 Daniel Francis	DB	5-11	179	Fr.	Port Barre	Port Barre
38 Gino Giambelluca	WR	5-8	173	So.	New Orleans	Holy Cross
39 Ryan Gaudet	PK	5-6	155	Fr.	New Orleans	Jesuit
40 Shawn Jordan	FB	6-2	242	Fr.	El Paso, Texas	Riverside
41 Chris Jackson	PK	5-11	159	Fr.	River Ridge	John Curtis
41 Marques Lewis	DB	5-8	176	Fr.	New Iberia	Westgate
42 Philip Maxwell	LB	6-1	220	So.	Shreveport	Evangel
43 Chad White	SS	5-11	211	Sr.	Hammond	Hammond
44 Kevin Steltz	FB	5-9	243	So.	New Orleans	Rummel
45 Willie Demps	LB	6-1	239	Fr.	Pensacola, Fla.	B. T. Washington
46 Cameron Vaughn	LB	6-4	220	So.	Terrytown	Shaw
47 Eric Edwards	TE	6-5	244	Sr.	Monroe	Ouachita Christian
48 Jarvus Ryes	DE	6-3	257	Jr.	Loreauville	Loreauville
48 Kirston Pittman	DE	6-3	238	Fr.	Reserve	East St. John
50 Jarrod Carter	DT	6-1	291	Fr.	River Ridge	John Curtis
51 Dominic Cooper	LB	6-4	220	Fr.	Metairie	O.P. Walker
52 Ryan Willis	DE	6-3	266	Fr.	New Orleans	Holy Cross
53 Joey Noto	LB	6-2	215	So.	Baton Rouge	Woodlawn
54 Brian West	LB	6-3	244	Fr.	West Monroe	West Monroe
55 Ben Wilkerson	C	6-4	296	Jr.	Hemphill, Texas	Hemphill
56 Kenneth Hollis	LB	6-0	241	Jr.	Adamsville, Ala.	East Miss. J.C.
57 Dave Peterson	LB	6-3	247	Sr.	Bristol, Fla.	Coffeyville CC
58 Lionel Turner	LB	6-2	257	Jr.	Walker	Walker
59 Doug Planchard	C	6-3	299	Fr.	Baton Rouge	Catholic
59 Leo Deselle	DL	6-0	265	Fr.	New Orleans	Shaw
60 Rodney Reed	OT	6-4	287	Sr.	West Monroe	West Monroe
61 Jimmy Courtenay	C	6-2	295	Sr.	New Orleans	Jesuit/Ole Miss
62 Harold Bicknell	OL	6-6	270	Jr.	Shreveport	Loyola
62 Brandon Hurley	OG	6-2	258	So.	Monroe	Ouachita Christian
63 Mac McLachlan	OT	6-4	314	Jr.	Kinder	Kinder
64 Rudy Niswanger	OL	6-5	294	So.	Monroe	Ouachita Christian
65 Steve Arflin	OG	6-4	300	So.	Jacksonville, Fla.	Fletcher
66 Jerry Sevin	OL	6-1	283	Fr.	River Ridge	John Curtis
68 Terrell McGill	OG	6-4	325	So.	Miami	Miami-Norland
69 Garett Wibel	OG	6-3	297	Fr.	Metairie	Rummel
70 Gant Petty	SNP	6-0	208	Fr.	Baton Rouge	Redemptorist
71 Nate Livings	OT	6-5	313	So.	Lake Charles	Washington-Marion
72 Stephen Peterman	OG	6-4	321	Sr.	Waveland, Miss.	St. Stanislaus
73 Will Arnold	OL	6-4	315	Fr.	Centreville, Miss.	Centreville
74 Josh Dicharry	OL	6-2	300	Fr.	Gonzales	East Ascension
75 Brian Johnson	OG	6-4	307	Fr.	Tallahassee, Fla.	Godby
76 Andrew Whitworth	OT	6-7	325	So.	West Monroe	West Monroe
77 Peter Dyakowski	OT	6-4	294	Fr.	Vancouver, B.C.	Vancouver Coll.
78 Paris Hodges	OT	6-5	329	Fr.	Vacaville, Calif.	Vanden
79 Sean Merrill	DE	6-3	255	Fr.	D'Iberville, Miss.	D'Iberville
80 Donnie Jones	P	6-3	222	Sr.	Baton Rouge	Catholic
80 Schirra Fields	WR	5-9	174	So.	Haynesville	Haynesville
81 Dwayne Bowe	WR	6-3	202	Fr.	Miami	Norland
82 David Jones	TE	6-4	259	So.	Silver Springs, Md.	Springbrook
83 Kory Hebert	TE	6-5	248	So.	Lafayette	Teurlings Catholic
84 Marcus Spears	DE	6-4	297	Jr.	Baton Rouge	Southern Lab
84 Andrew Wright	TE	6-7	238	Fr.	Lake Charles	Barbe
85 Craig Davis	WR	6-2	190	Fr.	New Orleans	O.P. Walker
86 Junior Joseph	WR	6-0	176	Fr.	New Orleans	O.P. Walker
86 Steve Damen	SNP	5-10	221	So.	Baton Rouge	Woodlawn
87 Blain Bech	WR	6-1	179	Fr.	Slidell	Slidell
88 Demetri Robinson	TE	6-3	251	Jr.	Lake City, Fla.	Columbia
89 Keith Zinger	TE	6-4	255	Fr.	Leesville	Leesville
90 Melvin Oliver	DT	6-3	269	So.	Opelika, Ala.	Opelika
91 Alonzo Manuel	LB	6-3	230	Fr.	Jennings	Jennings
92 Bryce Wyatt	DT	6-4	273	Sr.	Lake Charles	Barbe
93 Chad Lavalais	DT	6-3	292	Sr.	Marksville	Marksville
94 Marquise Hill	DE	6-7	295	Jr.	New Orleans	De La Salle
95 Kyle Williams	DT	6-2	288	So.	Ruston	Ruston
96 Carnell Stewart	DE	6-4	297	Fr.	River Ridge	John Curtis
97 Brandon Washington	DE	6-4	302	So.	Tuscaloosa, Ala.	Central
98 Torran Williams	DT	6-3	297	Sr.	Miami	Dodge
99 Jason LeDoux	ILB	6-3	228	Sr.	West Monroe	Texas A&M

TEAM MILESTONES (Statistics include the Sugar Bowl)

13 wins, most in school history

7 SEC wins, most in school history

475 points scored, most in school history (previous record: 375 in 1977)

63 touchdowns, most in school history (previous record: 51 in 1977)

252 yards allowed per game, No. 1 in the nation

33.9 points per game, second in school history (current record: 34.90 in 1969)

11 points allowed per game, No. 1 in the nation

HONORS ABOUND

Following LSU's success in 2003, many Tigers players and Coach Nick Saban were singled out for their efforts:

NICK SABAN, head coach
▶ National Coach of the Year (AP, CNNSI.com)
▶ SEC co-Coach of the Year (AP)

MICHAEL CLAYTON, WR
▶ Biletnikoff Award semifinalist
▶ Third team All-American (AP, Collegefootballnews.com)
▶ First-team All-SEC (AP, coaches, Collegefootballnews.com, ESPN.com)
▶ SEC's Top Receiver (Collegefootballnews.com)
▶ The 100 Best Players of 2003 — No. 44 (Collegefootballnews.com)

SKYLER GREEN, punt returner
▶ First-team All-American (CNNSI.com, ESPN.com)
▶ Second-team All-American (Collegefootballnews.com)
▶ Third-team All-American (AP)
▶ Honorable mention All-American (Rivals.com)
▶ First-team All-SEC (Collegefootballnews.com)
▶ Second-team All-SEC (AP, coaches)

DEVERY HENDERSON, WR
▶ Second-team All-SEC (AP, coaches)

DONNIE JONES, punter
▶ Ray Guy Award semifinalist

LARON LANDRY, safety
▶ First-team Freshman All-American (Collegefootballnews.com, Rivals.com)
▶ Second-team All-SEC (AP)
▶ Freshman All-SEC (coaches)

CHAD LAVALAIS, DT
▶ Lombardi Award finalist
▶ Nagurski Award finalist
▶ Outland Trophy finalist
▶ Walter Camp All-American
▶ First-team All-American (AP, CNNSI.com, Collegefootballnews.com, ESPN.com, FWAA, Rivals.com, Sporting News)
▶ First-team All-SEC (AP, coaches, Collegefootballnews.com, ESPN.com)
▶ SEC Player of the Year (Collegefootballnews.com)
▶ SEC's Top Defensive Lineman (Collegefootballnews.com)
▶ SEC Player of the Week (vs. Auburn — Oct. 25, vs. Ole Miss — Nov. 22)
▶ The 100 Best Players of 2003 — No. 8 (Collegefootballnews.com)

MATT MAUCK, QB
▶ Second-team All-SEC (AP, coaches)
▶ SEC Offensive Player of the Week (vs. Arkansas — Nov. 22)
▶ The 100 Best Players of 2003 — No. 75 (Collegefootballnews.com)

STEPHEN PETERMAN, OG
▶ Lombardi Award candidate
▶ First-team All-American (CNNSI.com, ESPN.com, Rivals.com, Sporting News)
▶ Second-team All-American (AP)
▶ First-team All-SEC (AP, Collegefootballnews.com)
▶ Second-team All-SEC (coaches)

KIRSTON PITTMAN, DE
▶ Honorable mention Freshman All-American (Collegefootballnews.com)

RODNEY REED, OT
▶ National Scholar-Athlete (National Football Foundation)

MARCUS SPEARS, DE
▶ First-team All-SEC (AP)

LIONEL TURNER, LB
▶ Honorable mention All-SEC (AP)

JUSTIN VINCENT, RB
▶ Sugar Bowl Most Outstanding Player
▶ SEC championship game Most Valuable Player
▶ First-team Freshman All-American (Rivals.com)
▶ Honorable mention Freshman All-American (Collegefootballnews.com)

COREY WEBSTER, CB
▶ Thorpe Award semifinalist
▶ Second-team All-American (AP, CNNSI.com, Collegefootballnews.com)
▶ Honorable mention All-American (Rivals.com)
▶ First-team All-SEC (AP, coaches, Collegefootballnews.com, ESPN.com)
▶ The 100 Best Players of 2003 — No. 56 (Collegefootballnews.com)
▶ National Defensive Player of the Week (vs. Georgia — Sept. 20)
▶ SEC Player of the Week (vs. Georgia — Sept. 20)

BEN WILKERSON, center
▶ Rimington Trophy candidate
▶ Second-team All-American (AP, Sporting News)
▶ Honorable Mention All-American (Rivals.com)
▶ First-team All-SEC (AP, ESPN.com)

KYLE WILLIAMS, DT
▶ Honorable mention All-SEC (AP)

KEITH ZINGER, TE
▶ Freshman All-SEC (coaches)

41 sacks, most in school history

7 defensive touchdowns, most in school history

PLAYER MILESTONES

(Statistics include the Sugar Bowl)

INDIVIDUAL CAREER RECORDS

MICHAEL CLAYTON, wide receiver
21 receiving touchdowns, most in school history
182 receptions, second in school history (current record: Wendell Davis, 183, 1984-87)
2,582 receiving yards, fourth in school history (current record: Josh Reed, 3,001, 1999-2001)

DEVERY HENDERSON, wide receiver
19 receiving touchdowns, tied for second in school history

MATT MAUCK, quarterback
37 passing touchdowns, third in school history (current record: Tommy Hodson, 69, 1986-89)

COREY WEBSTER, cornerback
14 interceptions, second in school history (current record: Chris Williams, 20, 1977-80)

DONNIE JONES, punter
234 punts, most in school history
9,798 punting yards, most in school history

INDIVIDUAL SINGLE-SEASON RECORDS

MATT MAUCK, quarterback
28 touchdown passes, most in school history (previous record: Tommy Hodson, 22, 1989)
2,825 passing yards, second in school history (current record: Rohan Davey, 3,347, 2001)

JUSTIN VINCENT, running back
1,001 rushing yards, most as a freshman in school history (previous record: Dalton Hillard, 901, 1982)

DEVERY HENDERSON, wide receiver
11 receiving touchdowns, tied for most in school history (Wendell Davis, 11, 1986)

MICHAEL CLAYTON, wide receiver
10 receiving touchdowns, tied for third in school history
78 receptions, third in school history (current record: Josh Reed, 94, 2001)

SKYLER GREEN, punt returner
462 punt return yards, fourth in school history (current record: Pinky Rohm, 539, 1937)

JEFF BOSS

MAY 1, 1949 — OCT. 27, 2003

LSU SPORTS INFORMATION

Longtime LSU equipment manager Jeff Boss died on Oct. 27, 2003, after a battle with brain cancer. He was 54.

Earlier that fall, the football team named the locker room in his honor and players placed "JB" on the back of their helmets to honor Boss, who had worked at LSU since 1980.

"These are great people; I really appreciate and love them dearly," Boss said during a ceremony Sept. 29 to christen the locker room.

Said LSU coach Nick Saban: "Jeff Boss was the best at what he did. He was without a doubt one of the absolute best people that you'd ever meet. You don't have many chances to meet someone who was as selfless as Jeff."

1958 GLORY REVISITED

PAUL DIETZEL, WHO COACHED LSU TO THE NATIONAL CHAMPIONSHIP 45 YEARS AGO, AND TIMES-PICAYUNE COLUMNIST PETER FINNEY, WHO COVERED THE TIGERS' RUN TO THE TOP THAT YEAR, LOOK BACK ON A LEGENDARY YEAR.

With a perfect season hanging in the balance, Mickey Mangham catches a 9-yard touchdown pass from running back Billy Cannon against Clemson in the Sugar Bowl on Jan. 1, 1959, in New Orleans. The Tigers prevailed 7-0, capping their 11-0 season.

In the days before the 2004 Nokia Sugar Bowl pairing LSU and Oklahoma, Times-Picayune Sports Editor David Meeks sat down over lunch with former Coach Paul Dietzel and columnist Peter Finney to reflect on the memorable '58 title run.

....

Coach, let's set the stage for 1958. Like many great coaching stories, this one begins with something that didn't happen — you almost becoming the head coach at Kentucky in 1954. If Blanton Collier — who accepted the job, had a change of heart and then again accepted it — had not become the Wildcats' coach, perhaps you never would've coached at LSU. Have you ever pondered that twist of fate?

DIETZEL: One of the great disappointments in my life at that time was when I arrived in Lexington only to find that Blanton had changed his mind and taken the job. And so we went back to West Point and, after another year, I ended up at LSU as the head coach. And guess who our opening game was? Kentucky. And I'll tell you what, I don't know if we ever had a team that was more ready to play. Our kids were so fired up because I was so fired up.

When you were hired at LSU, you were only 29 years old. You were the youngest coach on your staff, and it wasn't even your staff — you agreed to retain the staff of your predecessor, Gaynell Tinsley. How did that affect your mindset when you arrived at LSU?

DIETZEL: Oh, I don't know. They did allow me to bring in one coach, so I hired Bill Peterson, who was from Mansfield,

THE COACH AND THE COLUMNIST

STAFF PHOTO BY MATT ROSE

Finney and Dietzel reminisce over lunch in December 2003

Finney writing in the 1950s

Dietzel coaching in the late 1950s

Paul Dietzel was head football coach at LSU for seven seasons, from 1955 through 1961. He won two SEC championships, and three of his teams won nine or more games. But it is 1958 for which Dietzel is most recognized, when he installed a new offense and a three-platoon system, launching the Tigers to an 11-0 season and the national championship. He had come to Baton Rouge from West Point, where he was an assistant at Army, and previously he had spent two years under Paul "Bear" Bryant at Kentucky. He later coached at Army and South Carolina. Now retired, Dietzel lives in Baton Rouge with his wife, Ann.

Times-Picayune columnist Peter Finney has been a sports journalist since 1945, when he began working for The States, which later became The States-Item and merged with The Times-Picayune in 1980. Finney has been to hundreds of LSU games in his career and covered all of the Tigers' contests in 1958. His columns appear regularly in The Times-Picayune.

Ohio, where I grew up. ... But you have to understand, LSU really had a fine coaching staff. ... Unfortunately, I have a picture of that coaching staff, and of the eight coaches I'm the only one still alive. But what a great group of coaches — Raymond Didier, Pop Strange, George Terry, Bill Peterson,

Coach Paul Dietzel had lost to Florida three times in a row, but running back Billy Cannon, scoring a touchdown in the second quarter, and LSU turned back the Gators 10-7 on Oct. 25, 1958, at Tiger Stadium in Baton Rouge. With the win, the Tigers moved to 6-0.

LSU SPORTS INFORMATION

GAME 1 *Sept. 20 at Rice*

With the rain dissipating before the game, the Tigers and Owls, who had beaten LSU two consecutive years, open their seasons before a damp crowd of 45,000 in Houston. The Tigers are in command from the start, but coach Paul Dietzel senses LSU could do better.

LSU	7	6	6	7	26
RICE	0	0	0	6	6

GAME 2 *Sept. 27 at Alabama*

Coach Paul "Bear" Bryant, who inherits a 2-7-1 team, takes the reins with the Crimson Tide, but the Tigers aren't intimidated in Mobile, Ala. LSU comes on strong in the second half, led by the rushing of Billy Cannon.

LSU	0	0	7	6	13
ALABAMA	0	3	0	0	3

GAME 3 *Oct. 4 at Tiger Stadium*

Before 45,000 in their home opener, the Tigers face an opposition led by coach Sammy Baugh, who also was the quarterback on a TCU squad that edged LSU 3-2 in the Sugar Bowl on Jan. 1, 1936. The Tigers have a strong first half, behind the play of quarterback Warren Rabb, and quickly move on.

HARDIN-SIMMONS	0	6	0	0	6
LSU	13	7	0	0	20

GAME 4 *Oct. 10 at Miami (Fla.)*

Not since 1937 had an LSU team won four games in a row to open a season, but this Tigers team does just that. Following the victory, LSU moves up to ninth in both the AP and UPI polls.

LSU	6	7	8	20	41
MIAMI (FLA.)	0	0	0	0	0

GAME 5 *Oct. 18 at Tiger Stadium*

The Wildcats are overmatched before 65,000 in Baton Rouge. Talk of the "White team," "Go team" and the "Chinese Bandits" now runs rampant with Tigers fans.

KENTUCKY	7	0	0	0	7
LSU	7	6	13	6	32

GAME 6 *Oct. 25 at Tiger Stadium*

Coach Paul Dietzel had lost to the Gators three times in a row, but the Tigers avert the fourth when Tommy Davis makes a field goal late in the fourth quarter. Dietzel praises Florida, but he had more praise for his standout running back, Billy Cannon, who scores the Tigers' touchdown.

FLORIDA	0	0	0	7	7
LSU	0	7	0	3	10

GAME 7 *Nov. 1 at Tiger Stadium*

In the first sellout in the history of the 67,500-seat Tiger Stadium, the atmosphere is tense, but LSU stays the course. With coach Johnny Vaught directing the Rebels, LSU halts Ole Miss on five tries inside the 2-yard line in the second quarter.

OLE MISS	0	0	0	0	0
LSU	0	7	0	7	14

GAME 8 *Nov. 8 at Tiger Stadium*

Now ranked No. 1 by The Associated Press and No. 3 by UPI, the Tigers fall behind early, but the Blue Devils' lead is short lived. LSU finds its stride in the second quarter, and Duke has no answers.

DUKE	6	0	6	6	18
LSU	6	22	8	14	50

GAME 9 *Nov. 15 at Mississippi State*

Following heavy rain, the Bulldogs (3-4) are able to muddle their way to an early touchdown, but miss the extra-point attempt. On a fourth-and-goal situation, quarterback Warren Rabb connects with Billy Hendrix on a touchdown pass, and Tommy Davis' extra point provides the final margin.

LSU	0	0	7	0	7
MISS. ST.	0	6	0	0	6

GAME 10 *Nov. 22 at Tulane*

With one game against rival Tulane separating the Tigers from their first recognized national championship (in these days the wire services awarded their national championship trophies before the bowl games), LSU shows no mercy.

LSU	0	6	21	35	62
TULANE	0	0	0	0	0

GAME 11: SUGAR BOWL *Jan. 1, 1959, in New Orleans*

Before a then Southeastern Conference record crowd of 83,221, the Tigers complete a perfect season by defeating Clemson. On third-and-eight at the 9-yard line in the third quarter, Billy Cannon takes a handoff and connects with Mickey Mangham for a touchdown on a halfback pass.

CLEMSON	0	0	0	0	0
LSU	0	0	7	0	7

Charlie McClendon, Carl Maddox, Abner Wimberley. There's no way you could have a better staff than that or one that got along better.

Coming into that season, you were in the fourth year of your program. Your best team was the year before, 1957, when you were 5-5. LSU had not won an SEC championship in 22 years, hadn't even won four games in a row in 21 years. What did you think of your team's chances that year?

DIETZEL: Well, you know when you're young, you're gung-ho and I was so determined. I didn't know what a good job I had as an assistant at West Point until I'd been the head coach down at LSU for a couple of years. ... I don't know that I thought about what we could win. I knew we had to do with what we had, and we didn't have much. LSU had gotten very lax.

Peter, what did you think about the '58 team in the preseason, having seen LSU for a number of years?

FINNEY: Well, I thought they had a chance to win some games. I mean, (Billy) Cannon was coming up, and he was going to be a good player. Everybody knew that. You (Dietzel) had put in a new system, the wing-T, and nobody knew how the team would adapt. I don't know when, but I think you mentioned that it started to click in that game at Miami.

That was fairly early in the season, the fourth game, after your win over Hardin-Simmons.

DIETZEL: A tough battle. They threw the ball real well.

And a few weeks earlier you had beaten Alabama, in "Bear" Bryant's first year there.

DIETZEL: Yep, 13-3, and that really was the making of the Chinese Bandits, because in that game Cannon was running the ball about halfway through the first quarter, and running and snorting like he did, and several times they sort of collared him up. And he's fighting his way, and the ball popped out. An Alabama boy caught it on the fly, and he takes off.

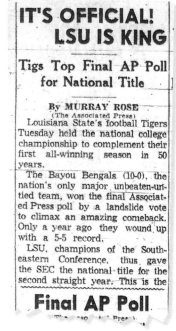

IT'S OFFICIAL! LSU IS KING

Tigs Top Final AP Poll for National Title

By MURRAY ROSE
(The Associated Press)

Louisiana State's football Tigers Tuesday held the national college championship to complement their first all-winning season in 50 years.

The Bayou Bengals (10-0), the nation's only major unbeaten-untied team, won the final Associated Press poll by a landslide vote to climax an amazing comeback. Only a year ago they wound up with a 5-5 record.

LSU, champions of the Southeastern Conference, thus gave the SEC the national title for the second straight year. This is the

Final AP Poll

We finally knocked him out of bounds ... at the 3-yard line. Well, I was sure they were going to score, and I'd rather not have our White team (first team) get discouraged, so I took them out and put in the Bandits (third team). ... They held them for three downs and made them kick a field goal. From that time on, I'll guarantee you, the Bandits thought they were pretty good.

Pete, obviously at that time you'd never seen three platoons of players. What were the guys in the press box saying about LSU's three-team system?

FINNEY: People weren't really conscious of it. I mean, they knew what was going on. I remember talking to (Dietzel) about it after the Alabama game, and you told me how you'd come up with the Chinese Bandits name out of a comic strip, and you really wanted to juice up the Bandits because it was this underweight group. I wrote this glowing report, and I remember the headline was, "LSU held up by Bandits."

And you stuck with the Bandits all year to rest your starters?

DIETZEL: We did, and it was a few weeks later after the Miami game that all of us coaches said, 'You know, we've got a pretty good football team. We may be a lot better than people think we are.'

Then you played Kentucky. It was supposed to be a tough game, but you won easily. At that point you had to be thinking this was your chance to make a run.

DIETZEL: At that point the only thing I was thinking was we had to get ready to make a run at the next team we were playing.

After squeaking past Florida, next came the game of the year — Ole Miss. LSU finally was ranked No. 1, Ole Miss also was undefeated, ranked No. 6. Peter, that had to be one of the bigger games you've ever seen.

FINNEY: Oh, no question. The big thing in that game was the goal-line stand. It was a scoreless game at the time, and I know Bobby Franklin, the Ole Miss quarterback, declined a

1958 LSU ROSTER

Number, Name	Pos.	Hgt	Wgt	Class	Hometown
10 Darryl Jenkins	QB	6-1	163	So.	Franklinton
11 Elton Upshaw	QB	6-1	190	So.	Monroe
12 Warren Rabb	QB	6-0	188	Jr.	Baton Rouge
14 E. Charbonnet	QB	further information unavailable			
16 Durel Matherne	QB	5-11	185	Jr.	Lutcher
20 Billy Cannon	HB	6-1	200	Jr.	Baton Rouge
21 Tommy Neck	HB	5-11	180	So.	Marksville
22 Hart Bourque	HB	5-8	175	So.	Gonzales
23 Don Purvis	HB	5-7	160	Jr.	Crystal Springs, Miss.
24 Ken McMichael	HB	5-11	190	So.	Minden
30 Frank Pannebaker	FB	5-10	205	So.	Mifflin, Pa.
31 Al Ott	HB	5-9	165	So.	Gretna
32 Henry Lee Roberts	HB	6-0	165	So.	Little Rock, Ark.
33 Donnie Daye	HB	5-10	180	So.	Ferriday
34 Johnny Robinson	HB	6-0	185	Jr.	Baton Rouge
40 J.W. Brodnax	FB	6-0	198	Sr.	Bastrop
41 Charles Tarter	FB	further information unavailable			
43 Merle Schexnaildre	FB	5-9	175	Jr.	Houma
44 Tommy Davis	FB	6-0	200	Jr.	Shreveport
50 Bob Greenwood	C	5-10	190	So.	Lake Charles
51 Max Fugler	C	6-1	198	Jr.	Ferriday
52 Ken Wittman	C	5-11	190	So.	Pass Christian, Miss.
53 John Langan	C	6-0	180	Jr.	Carbondale, Ill.
54 John Dunham	C	6-4	229	So.	Shreveport
55 George O'Neal	C	further information unavailable			
60 Fred Davidson	G	6-1	190	So.	New Iberia
61 Tommy Lott	G	5-9	190	Jr.	Texarkana, Ark.
62 Manson Nelson	G	5-9	180	Jr.	Ferriday
63 Al Dampier	G	6-1	200	So.	Clayton
64 Larry Kahlden	G	6-1	204	Sr.	Weimar, Texas
65 Emile Fournet	G	5-11	202	Jr.	Bogalusa
66 Mike Stupka	G	6-0	205	Jr.	Bogalusa
67 Ed McCreedy	G	6-1	205	So.	Biloxi, Miss.
68 Herb Lacassagne	T	6-2	210	So.	New Orleans
69 Gerald Frey	G	5-11	210	So.	Iota
70 Lynn LeBlanc	T	6-2	200	Jr.	Crowley
71 Duane Leopard	T	6-2	205	Jr.	Baton Rouge
72 Charles "Bo" Strange	T	6-1	205	So.	Baton Rouge
73 Jack Frayer	T	6-2	215	Jr.	Toledo, Ohio
74 Dave McCarty	T	6-2	190	Jr.	Rayville
75 Mel Branch	T	6-1	200	Jr.	DeRidder
76 Bob Richards	T	6-2	210	So.	Oak Ridge, Tenn.
77 Carroll Bergeron	T	6-0	215	So.	Houma
78 Joe Dosher	T	6-4	215	So.	Jena
79 Gus Riess	T	6-0	215	So.	New Orleans
80 Andy Bourgeois	E	5-10	180	So.	New Orleans
81 Gaynell Kinchen	E	6-3	190	So.	Baton Rouge
82 Don Norwood	E	6-3	200	Jr.	Baton Rouge
83 Scotty McClain	E	6-2	185	Jr.	Smackover, Ark.
84 Jimmy Bond	E	6-1	190	So.	Bogalusa
85 Billy Hendrix	E	6-0	185	Sr.	Rayville
86 Mickey Mangham	E	6-1	190	So.	Kensington, Md.
87 Jimmy Givens	E	6-1	190	Jr.	Bogalusa
88 David Parish	E	6-3	200	So.	Hammond
89 Fred Blankenship	E	6-4	199	So.	North Little Rock, Ark.

penalty because with the play they had the ball 12 inches from the goal line and they thought they couldn't be stopped. LSU held and later ended up scoring twice to win the game. But I think it was that goal-line stand really broke Ole Miss.

Any similarities between the '58 team and the current LSU team, in the way they play?

DIETZEL: Well, keep in mind that if someone had come out and lined up against us with four wideouts back then, we'd call timeout. We wouldn't know what to do. Our defensive coaches would've said, 'They don't have anyone in the back-field. What's going on?' The game has changed tremendously. ... But someone told me, because I had forgotten, how few points we gave up in '58, and how this LSU team hasn't allowed a lot of points. So the defenses were both pretty good. I mean, we only allowed 53 points that year in 11 games. If we got a touchdown and a field goal, the game was over. We shut a lot of people out. We just absolutely would not let anyone score on us. I'll say this: In 1958 and '59, we were as good a football team as there was anywhere. And in 2003, Nick Saban's LSU team is as fine a team as there is anywhere. I truly believe that.

FIGHTING SPIRIT A TRADEMARK OF McCLENDON'S TIGERS

PETER FINNEY

No pretense. Ever.

"The worst mistake any coach can make is not being himself," Charlie McClendon liked to say, a credo that shaped the man and his accomplishments.

McClendon sprinkled his Arkansas brogue with "gosh knows" — he made no attempts at histrionics — and his honesty in a profession given to double-talk was amazing as well as refreshing.

The coach refused to stray from his roots, a reflection of his humble origin, the tiny community of Lewisville, Ark., a short distance from Fordyce, birthplace of the sainted Paul "Bear" Bryant.

"Fordyce was so far back in the country," Bryant was fond of saying, "that when we moved, all we had to do was throw water on the fire and call the dogs."

Charlie Mac was the eighth, and last, child born to a struggling family and, as he told it, it was a miracle he lived to coach LSU for 18 seasons. His mother came within a whisker of dying when she gave birth, creating a chaotic scene, the sight of Doc Youmans (Mac's middle name) working to keep the mother alive while ignoring the newly born.

"Doc Youmans had a choice of working on me or mama," McClendon said. "He figured seven kids needed a mom more than another child. So he put me on the other side of the bed and tended to her. I had to fight for myself."

LSU SPORTS INFORMATION

Charlie McClendon, who coached 18 years at LSU, leaves the field a victor in his final LSU game, a 34–10 victory against Wake Forest in the Tangerine Bowl on Dec. 22, 1979, in Orlando, Fla.

That was the story of Charlie Mac — the guy who kept on fighting.

McClendon, who died in 2001 at age 78, counted tenacity, persistence and loyalty among his many memorable attributes. Here was a guy who did not play football in high school because there were not enough players to field a team, who won a football scholarship to Magnolia A&M (later known as Southern Arkansas University) and then to Kentucky.

He played end for Bryant's finest Kentucky team, the 1950 Wildcats who upset No. 1 Oklahoma in the Sugar Bowl, a game in which Bryant remembered McClendon for being "bloody but unbowed."

"Early in the game," Bryant recalled in his biography, "Charlie McClendon came off the field with the side of his face torn off. When I turned to call the trainer and looked around, he was already going back on the field with the defense. His tackling caused three fumbles that day."

As it turned out, Charlie Mac was just being Charlie Mac — a survivor against the odds. As a Kentucky assistant, he struck up a friendship with another Kentucky assistant, Paul Dietzel. Later, as an LSU assistant, he talked Dietzel into applying for the LSU job following the firing of Gaynell Tinsley.

When LSU won the national championship under Dietzel in 1958, Charlie Mac was the coordinator of the Tigers' famed defense.

When Dietzel departed for West Point after the '61 season, Charlie Mac was the obvious choice to replace him at LSU. But it was still a fight. Two years earlier, Mac had "shaken hands" on the Navy job and returned from Annapolis whistling "Anchors Aweigh." But he didn't get the job.

Now Charlie Mac was waiting once again, waiting for LSU athletic director Jim Corbett to make a decision on Dietzel's successor.

But when Kentucky offered Charlie Mac their head coaching job, Corbett moved quickly and hired McClendon.

Taking over with high expectations and a rugged schedule, McClendon quipped, "The schedule is big, but we've never lost a game before we played it."

Charlie Mac went on to win nearly 70 percent of his games, coached 17 All-Americans, took the Tigers to 13 bowl games, was a two-time SEC Coach of the Year and national Coach of the Year in 1973.

In 18 seasons at LSU, the Tigers had 16 winning seasons. McClendon is the winningest coach in LSU football history, with a career mark of 137-59-7. Two of his biggest victories came in the Cotton Bowl, upsets of Texas in '63 and Arkansas in '66. McClendon also led LSU to a pair of wins in the Sugar Bowl (1965 and '68).

As fate would have it, McClendon died the day before Nick Saban led LSU to a win over Tennessee in the 2001 SEC championship game.

In one of his final interviews, McClendon was asked to name his biggest victory. There was no hesitation.

"Getting Dorothy Faye to marry an ugly guy like me," he said, reminding you that Dorothy Faye Smart, his wife of 53 years, was the loveliest coed on the campus at Magnolia A&M. "I could never figure that one out."

STAFF FILE PHOTO

Coach Charlie McClendon prepares the Tigers, who had won the SEC title, for their matchup against Nebraska in the Orange Bowl in Miami. LSU fell to the Cornhuskers 17-12 on Jan. 1, 1970, but McClendon, who finished with a 137-59-7 record, still is revered in Baton Rouge.

LSU
21

OKLAHOMA
14

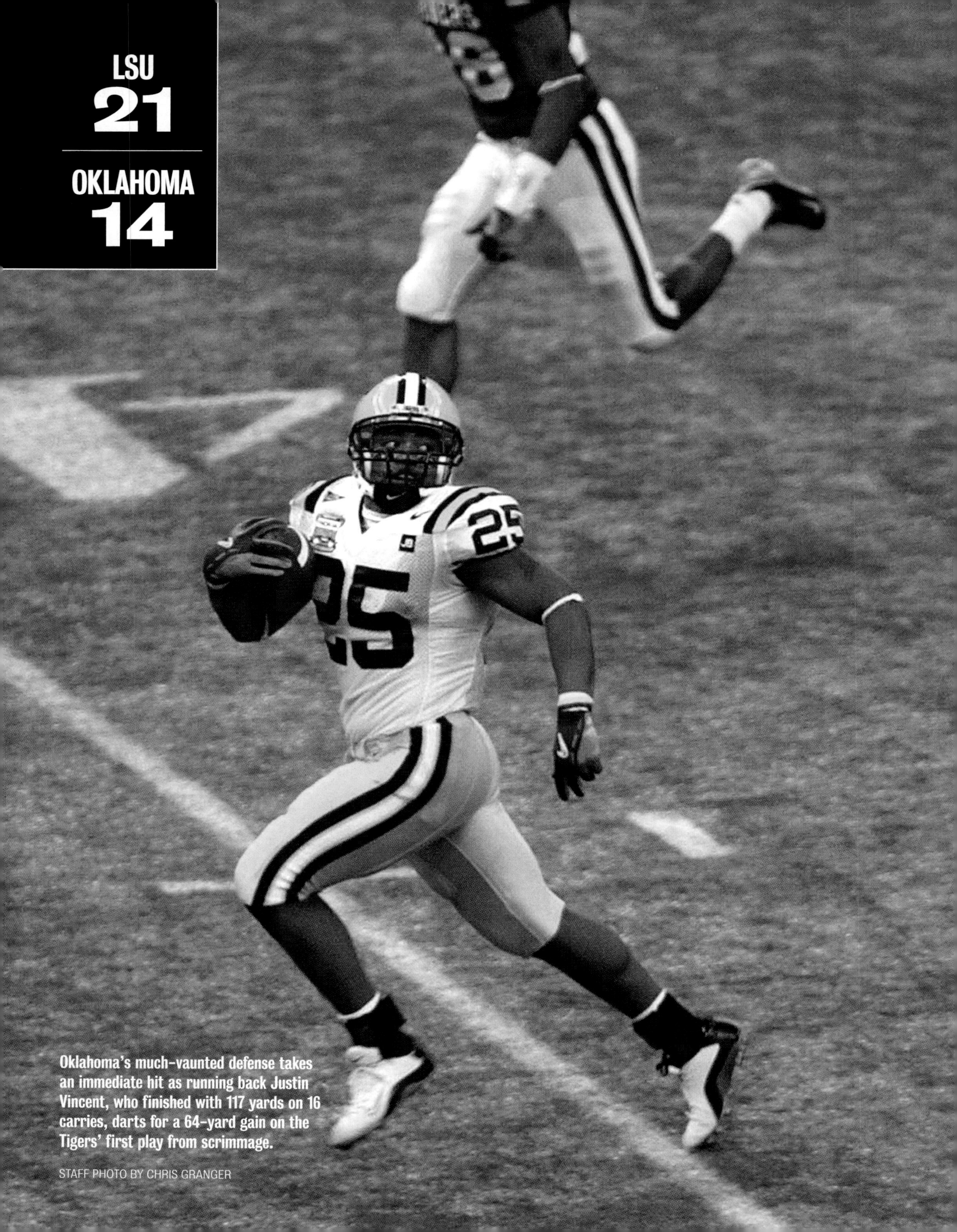

Oklahoma's much-vaunted defense takes an immediate hit as running back Justin Vincent, who finished with 117 yards on 16 carries, darts for a 64-yard gain on the Tigers' first play from scrimmage.

STAFF PHOTO BY CHRIS GRANGER

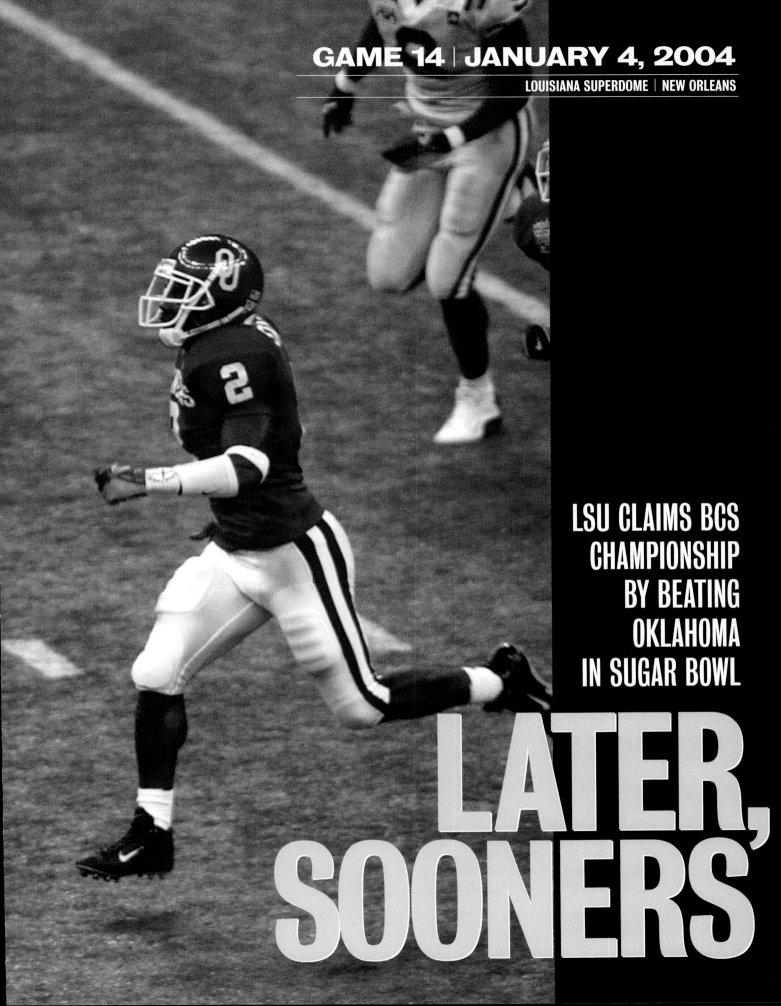

LSU CLAIMS BCS
CHAMPIONSHIP
BY BEATING
OKLAHOMA
IN SUGAR BOWL

LATER,
SOONERS

LSU 21
OKLAHOMA 14

RECORD CROWD SEES TIGERS CLAIM NATIONAL TITLE

BY MIKE TRIPLETT STAFF WRITER

Claiming their place among the greatest accomplishments in Louisiana sports history, the LSU Tigers thrilled a Superdome-record crowd with a 21-14 victory over the Oklahoma Sooners in the 2004 Nokia Sugar Bowl to wrap up the school's first national championship in 45 years.

As if the victory wasn't enough, there was the dramatic finish. An entire state exhaled when LSU's defense finally secured the victory — as it had done all season.

The Tigers (13-1) jumped to a 21-7 lead, then hung on for the final two quarters to turn away the Sooners, who came into the game ranked No. 1 in the Bowl Championship Series standings.

But LSU changed that, and the USA Today/ESPN coaches' poll made it official shortly after the game, ranking the Tigers No. 1 with 60 of 63 first-place votes. LSU also took home the coveted national champion's crystal trophy, showing it to the

With defensive tackle Chad Lavalais, left, wide receiver Michael Clayton, second from left, and the rest of the Tigers surrounding him, Coach Nick Saban accepts the crystal BCS championship trophy after defeating the Sooners. LSU hadn't won a national title in football since 1958.

STAFF PHOTO BY ALEX BRANDON

With Oklahoma trailing 14-7, quarterback Jason White (18) isn't able to prevent LSU defensive end Marcus Spears from scoring on a 20-yard interception return on the Sooners' first series in the third quarter.

Superdome throng and passing it around on the field, from Coach Nick Saban to receiver Michael Clayton, defensive tackle Chad Lavalais and cornerback Corey Webster.

Southern California, as expected, was ranked No. 1 in The Associated Press writers' poll after finishing 12-1 with a victory in the Rose Bowl. The Trojans received 48 first-place votes in that poll, while the Tigers got 17.

No one associated with LSU was even slightly concerned about the split title. And Saban said the joy the Tigers' sea-

son had brought to its faithful made it all worthwhile.

"What makes me happy about doing this is seeing how it makes so many people happy," Saban said — after admitting he was already trying to figure out how the Tigers could repeat their success next season.

The game took place in front of the largest crowd to witness a sporting event in the storied Superdome — 79,342, at least three-fourths of them donning purple and gold. But the place was eerily quiet with five minutes remaining, with

STAFF PHOTO BY CHUCK COOK

Oklahoma quarterback Jason White has nowhere to go as LSU defensive tackle Melvin Oliver (90) lowers the boom.

STAFF PHOTO BY CHRIS GRANGER

Defensive backs Jack Hunt (8) and Corey Webster thwart the efforts of Oklahoma wide receiver Will Peoples in the first quarter. Webster was able to come up with the interception to get LSU back on track.

Oklahoma driving and LSU's defense, for the first time all game, showing signs of wear. The Tigers fans must have forgotten for a moment that their team's best unit was on the field.

LSU's defense stopped Heisman Trophy-winning quarterback Jason White on four straight passes inside the 10-yard line.

The fourth-and-goal play with 2:52 remaining was the most dramatic. White locked in on receiver Mark Clayton in the end zone, but LSU freshman safety Jessie Daniels knocked the ball away.

"They were in our territory. We just wanted to make a stand any way we could," Webster said. "So we came through

and stopped them right there. They didn't like it when you hit them in the nose. We did that tonight, and they backed off."

Bob Stoops said LSU's defense was the best he has faced in his five seasons as Oklahoma's coach. His team, which led the nation in scoring this year (45.2 points per game), had gained just 79 yards through three quarters and finished with 154.

Oklahoma got the ball back with 2:09 remaining at its 49-yard line. But White threw three more incomplete passes before being sacked on fourth down by LSU linebacker Lionel Turner.

"We got tired at the end. But we played from the heart.

LSU wide receiver Skyler Green catches a 23-yard pass but is tackled at Oklahoma's 5-yard line by safety Brodney Pool.

We played with our identity," Saban said. "And I love these kids."

The deciding touchdown, fittingly, came from LSU's defense. On the first play after halftime, White was sacked by defensive end Marcus Spears for a 3-yard loss.

On the second play after halftime, White's pass was intercepted by Spears, who returned the ball for a 20-yard touchdown and a 21-7 lead.

White completed 13 of 37 passes for 102 yards, no touchdowns and two interceptions. He was sacked five times.

LSU entered the game as a 6½-point underdog — mostly because Oklahoma was supposed to have the better offense. But the Tigers showed their firepower first when, on the game's first play from scrimmage, freshman tailback Justin Vincent broke loose for a 64-yard run.

LSU did not score on the drive, because quarterback Matt Mauck fumbled on the 1-yard line. But, true to form, the Tigers' defense got the ball right back. On White's first pass, he dropped back into the end zone, heaved the ball up for grabs, and Webster intercepted at the Oklahoma 49-yard line.

Three plays later, LSU receiver Skyler Green scored on a

STAFF PHOTO BY TED JACKSON

With the clock winding down, running back Barrington Edwards roars his approval as the Tigers turn back the Sooners before a jubilant crowd at the Superdome.

FINAL AP POLL	
RANK, SCHOOL	**PREVIOUS**
1. SOUTHERN CAL (48*)	1
2. LSU (17*)	2
3. OKLAHOMA	3
4. OHIO STATE	7
5. MIAMI (FLA.)	10
6. MICHIGAN	4
7. GEORGIA	11
8. IOWA	13
9. WASHINGTON STATE	15
10. MIAMI (OHIO)	14

* first-place votes
Released Jan. 5, 2004

FINAL COACHES POLL	
RANK, SCHOOL	**PREVIOUS**
1. LSU (60*)	2
2. SOUTHERN CAL (3*)	1
3. OKLAHOMA	3
4. OHIO STATE	6
5. MIAMI (FLA.)	9
6. GEORGIA	11
7. MICHIGAN	4
8. IOWA	12
9. WASHINGTON STATE	14
10. FLORIDA STATE	8

24-yard end around.

Oklahoma tied the score at 7 after blocking an LSU punt in the second quarter and recovering on the Tigers' 2-yard line. Three plays later, tailback Kejuan Jones ran it in from the 1.

But LSU responded with an eight-play, 80-yard touchdown drive. Vincent rushed 18 yards for the score.

"That was the turning point of the game," Saban said. "They blocked a punt and scored, and our offense came right back and scored."

Vincent, who ran for 117 yards on 16 carries, was selected the game's Most Outstanding Player — repeating his honor from the SEC championship game.

Oklahoma scored its final touchdown with 11 minutes remaining on another 1-yard run by Jones. The Sooners began that drive on LSU's 31-yard line after safety Brodney Pool intercepted a pass by Mauck and returned the ball 49 yards.

Mauck completed 13 of 22 passes for 124 yards, no touchdowns and two interceptions.

But a seven-point victory was enough for LSU. And it was pointed out to Saban that, while many people believed USC should've been in the Sugar Bowl instead of Oklahoma, no one disputed LSU's right to be in the game.

"You know what," Saban said. "I never ever said that. But I always believed it.

"I believed in these guys, and they believed in each other."

LSU	7	7	7	0	21
OKLAHOMA	0	7	0	7	14

SCORING SUMMARY

LSU Skyler Green 24-yard run (Ryan Gaudet kick). Three plays, 32 yards in 1:09

OKLAHOMA Kejuan Jones 1-yard run (Trey DiCarlo kick). Three plays, two yards in 1:04

LSU Justin Vincent 18-yard run (Gaudet kick). Nine plays, 80 yards in 3:10

LSU Marcus Spears 20-yard interception return (Gaudet kick)

OKLAHOMA Jones 1-yard run (DiCarlo kick). Nine plays, 31 yards in 3:45

TEAM STATISTICS

CATEGORY	OKLAHOMA	LSU
FIRST DOWNS	12	13
RUSHES-YARDS (NET)	33-52	40-159
PASSING YDS (NET)	102	153
PASSES ATT-COMP-INT	37-13-2	24-14-2
TOTAL OFFENSE PLAYS-YARDS	70-154	64-312
PUNT RETURNS-YARDS	5-36	3-26
KICKOFF RETURNS-YARDS	2-24	0-0
PUNTS (NUMBER-AVG)	8-45.9	8-34.0
FUMBLES-LOST	2-0	1-1
PENALTIES-YARDS	11-70	8-65
POSSESSION TIME	28:41	31:19
SACKS BY (NUMBERS-YARDS)	5-12	5-46

INDIVIDUAL OFFENSIVE STATISTICS

RUSHING: **LSU** — Justin Vincent 16-117; Matt Mauck 14-27; Skyler Green 3-22; Alley Broussard 2-6; Joseph Addai 2 minus-1; team 3 minus-12. **Oklahoma** — Kejuan Jones 20-59; Mark Clayton 4-38; Renaldo Works 1-2; team 1 minus-1; Jason White 7 minus-46

PASSING: **LSU** — Matt Mauck 13-22-2-124; Blain Bech 1-1-0-29; Michael Clayton 0-1-0-0. **Oklahoma** — Jason White 13-37-2-102

RECEIVING: **LSU** — Michael Clayton 4-38; David Jones 3-54; Devery Henderson 2-24; Skyler Green 2-23; Joseph Addai 2-12; Eric Edwards 1-2. **Oklahoma** — Mark Clayton 4-32; Travis Wilson 3-31; J.D. Runnels 2-19; Kejuan Jones 2-6; Mark Bradley 1-9; Brandon Jones 1-5

INDIVIDUAL DEFENSIVE STATISTICS

INTERCEPTIONS: **LSU** — Corey Webster 1-18; Marcus Spears 1-20. **Oklahoma** — Antoni Perkins 1-13; Brodney Pool 1-49

SACKS (unassisted, assisted): **LSU** — Lionel Turner 2-0; Melvin Oliver 1-0; Marcus Spears 1-0; Marquise Hill 1-0. **Oklahoma** — Tommie Harris 1-0; Brodney Pool 1-0; Dan Cody 1-0; Teddy Lehman 1-0; Donte Nicholson 1-0

TACKLES (unassisted, assisted): **LSU** — Lionel Turner 8-1; Eric Alexander 5-3; Jack Hunt 4-2; Chad Lavalais 4-0; Melvin Oliver 4-0; Marquise Hill 3-1; Travis Daniels 2-2; Kyle Williams 2-1; Marcus Spears 2-0; LaRon Landry 1-3; Michael Clayton 1-0; Jesse Daniels 1-0; Cameron Vaughn 1-1; Gant Petty 1-0; Bennie Brazell 1-0; David Jones 1-0; Chad White 1-0; Brian West 0-1; Randall Gay 0-1. **Oklahoma** — Brodney Pool 8-2; Derrick Strait 8-3; Donte Nicholson 6-1; Teddy Lehman 5-3; Gayron Allen 3-1; Jonathan Jackson 3-1; Antonio Perkins 3-0; Tommie Harris 2-1; Brandon Everage 1-0; Brandon Shelby 1-0; Dan Cody 1-1; Dusty Dvoracek 1-0; J.D. Runnels 1-0; Will Peoples 1-0; Pasha Jackson 0-1

STAR-STUDDED CAST CARRIES TIGERS TO THE TOP

BY PETER FINNEY
COLUMNIST

Move over Trojans, there's a Tiger in the room.

A bunch of Tigers.

There's Lionel Turner, a blitzing linebacker, who flattened the Oklahoma kid who won the Heisman Trophy, Jason White, to sew up a 21-14 victory that gave LSU another trophy, the crystal football as the BCS champion of the planet.

There's Marcus Spears, who carried 297 pounds into the end zone with an interception that gave the Tigers their winning cushion.

There's Marquise Hill, another cat-quick defensive end, who made life miserable for the guys in red all evening long, knocking down passes and drilling ball carriers.

And there are those tireless speedsters in the secondary, Randall Gay and Eric Alexander and Corey Webster and Travis Daniels, who are either going for the quarterback's jugular or are running downfield tossing blankets on receivers.

The Tigers' Skyler Green reaches the end zone on a 24-yard end around in the first quarter to open the scoring.

STAFF PHOTO BY ELIOT KAMENITZ

With the Sooners facing fourth-and-10 with 1:51 remaining in the fourth quarter, Tigers linebacker Lionel Turner sacks Jason White to seal Oklahoma's fate.

STAFF PHOTO BY CHRIS GRANGER

Finally, there was Justin Vincent, whose 117 rushing yards made him the game's Most Outstanding Player, just as his 201 yards against Georgia made him the MVP of the SEC championship game.

The case can be made that LSU kept the Sooners in the game, first with a penalty that erased a field goal that would have put the Tigers up by 17 in the third quarter, later with an interception of an errant throw by Matt Mauck that set up the score that pulled the Sooners to within a touchdown.

It was fitting that Nick Saban's Tigers won a national championship with one defensive stop after another, a tribute to the architect who has made defense a mission, who has developed a disciplined consistency that has carried his ballclub to the heights all teams dream about.

Consider this: Saban's defense held a team that averaged 461 yards over the season to 154 yards — 52 yards of it rushing. LSU limited a team that averaged 45 points to a couple of touchdowns, one on a 2-yard drive after a blocked punt, another on a 31-yard push following an interception.

They made a virtual basket case of White, who was picked off twice, who struggled to complete 13 passes in 37 tries. They closed the rushing lanes, they made their blitzes pay off, and they never stopped coming.

Most significantly, they kept responding to adversity, which they've managed to do all year.

On the game's first play, there went Vincent popping up the middle, juking linebacker Gayron Allen five yards past the line of scrimmage, then setting sail for the end zone. What looked for a moment like an 80-yard touchdown gallop turned into a more modest one of 64 yards when a streaking Derrick Strait ran down the freshman on the Sooners' 16.

Four plays later, the Tigers were playing a first-and-goal at

STAFF PHOTO BY ALEX BRANDON

LSU guard Stephen Peterman (72) and linebacker Lionel Turner know who's No. 1 after Turner sacked Jason White on fourth-and-10 with 1:51 remaining.

the 1 when Mauck could not handle the snap and fumbled it away at the 2.

Whereupon, two plays later, Webster picked off a bomb launched by White at midfield and returned it to the Sooners' 32. It took LSU four plays to punch it in, which Skyler Green did by turning right end and scooting along the sideline from the 24.

The Tigers had made their first response. The second came after Oklahoma blocked a second-quarter punt and got life two yards away from the end zone. But it took the Sooners one-two-three-four plays (after a penalty) to punch it in.

An Oklahoma offense that had scored on its first possession 11 times during the season, and twice on its second, wound up moving two yards for its only first-half points, and they didn't do it until the Sooners' fifth offensive series.

The Sooners had been outgained 204-50, and yet they had managed to tie at 7-7.

But back came the Tigers, this time with an 80-yard drive that had Mauck throwing strikes to Devery Henderson, Michael Clayton and David Jones, after which Vincent applied the exclamation point with another up-the-gut explosion, this one from 18 yards.

That was the story.

Response.

Defense.

Championship.

We'll never know how these Tigers could have done against Southern Cal, No. 1 in the media poll, in a season that will produce split champions.

Nick Saban could not care less. To him, all that matters is the crystal football that will be sitting in LSU's trophy case.

"The crowd was unbelievable," Saban said. "I can't think of a better city for LSU to win a national championship."

Defensive tackle Chad Lavalais, left, and wide receiver Michael Clayton are loving it after the Tigers defeated the Sooners in the Sugar Bowl to claim the BCS championship game trophy.

STAFF PHOTO BY ALEX BRANDON

STAFF PHOTO BY ALEX BRANDON

Defensive end Marcus Spears reacts after scoring on a 20-yard interception return early in the third quarter, but the Tigers' defense still had work to do before LSU emerged as No. 1.

STAFF PHOTO BY ALEX BRANDON

After the Tigers' victory over the Sooners in the BCS championship game, defensive tackle Chad Lavalais revels in the moment as LSU caps a 13-1 season and wins its first national title in football since 1958.

STAFF PHOTO BY MICHAEL DEMOCKER

To the victors go the spoils. Wide receiver Michael Clayton raises the BCS championship game crystal trophy after LSU defeats Oklahoma in the Sugar Bowl on Jan. 4 at the Superdome.

STAFF PHOTO BY ELIOT KAMENITZ

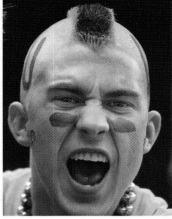

STAFF PHOTO BY TED JACKSON

STAFF PHOTO BY TED JACKSON

Above, when it comes to cheering on the Tigers, these two fans not only know which team is No. 1, but they also show their stripes.

Top, Deafening. That is the best way to describe the noise level the LSU and Oklahoma fans produced at the BCS championship game.

Left, the Golden Band From Tigerland has the crowd in a frenzy before the start of the BCS title game between LSU and Oklahoma.

CROWD PLEASER
LSU WR Clayton dazzles fans and ULM in Tigers' season opener

Trojans dominate Auburn

LSU makes triumphant comeback

Saints have unanswered questions

AUG. 31, 2003

HAPPY ENDING
Tigers come up with big plays late to beat No. 7 Georgia

Wave outlasts Army

Tigers, Mauck don't crack when going gets tough

Mauck overcomes fumble to throw winning TD pass

Saints, Titans are physical

Ten Most Wanted triumphs in close-run Super Derby

SEPT. 21, 2003

A DARK LESSON
Saban's words fall on deaf ears as Tigers suffer season's first loss

Cougars take control early, hold off Wave

Overconfident LSU gets caught looking ahead

Sluggish Tigers collapse against game Gators

Haslett staying level-headed, cool under fire

Scrappy Hornets fall short

OCT. 12, 2003

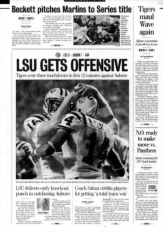

Beckett pitches Marlins to Series title

LSU GETS OFFENSIVE
Tigers score three touchdowns in first 12 minutes against Auburn

Tigers maul Wave again

N.O. ready to make move vs. Panthers

LSU delivers key knockout punch in outclassing Auburn

Coach Saban credits players for getting a total team win

OCT. 26, 2003

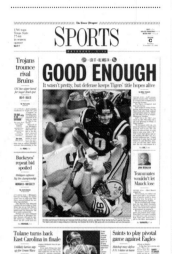

GOOD ENOUGH
It wasn't pretty, but defense keeps Tigers' title hopes alive

Trojans trounce rival Bruins

Buckeyes' repeat bid spoiled

Teammates wouldn't let Mauck lose

Tulane turns back East Carolina in finale

Saints to play pivotal game against Eagles

NOV. 23, 2003

ON TO ATLANTA
Tigers rout Razorbacks and turn their attention to the SEC championship game

LSU hopes to have changed some minds

'Bigger challenge' is next for Tigers

Crowds and expectations usually are elevated for Tigers-Jaguars

NYC's Madison Square Garden is the apple of the Hornets' eyes

NOV. 29, 2003

STATEMENT MADE
Tigers win convincingly, wait for final BCS poll today

K-State stuns Sooners; BCS in disarray

The question should be: Who of Tigers face for bigger Bowl?

USC GRABS VICTORY

Floyd shows Chicago his coaching skills

Saints seek December worth remembering

DEC. 7, 2003

HOW SWEET!
LSU TO PLAY OKLAHOMA IN BCS CHAMPIONSHIP GAME

Being good not always good enough

City budget depending on Santa Claus

Tigers earn stripes with awesome run and a strong finish

DEC. 8, 2003

The Times-Picayune

50 CENTS   166th year   No. 347   MONDAY, JANUARY 5, 2004   METRO EDITION

21 TIGERS   SOONERS 14

LSU No.1

SUGAR BOWL VICTORY GIVES TIGERS FIRST TITLE SINCE 1958

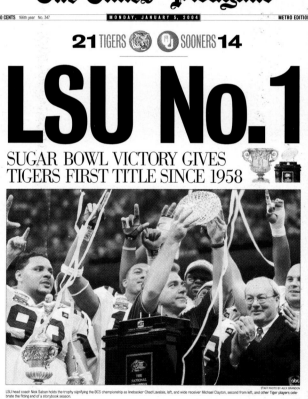

LSU head coach Nick Saban holds the trophy signifying the BCS championship as linebacker Chad Lavalais, left, and wide receiver Michael Clayton, second from left, and other Tiger players celebrate the fitting end of a storybook season.

SUGAR BOWL COVERAGE INSIDE
▶ Fans swarm to the game, A-6
▶ 16 pages of game coverage, Section D

Total team effort puts Tigers on top

PETER FINNEY

Move over TrojanFs, there's a Tiger in the room.

A bunch of Tigers.

There's Lionel Turner, a blitzing linebacker, who flattened the Oklahoma kid who won the Heisman, Jason White, to see up a 21-14 victory that gave LSU another trophy, the crystal football as the BCS champion of the planet.

There's Marcus Spears, who carried 297 pounds into the end zone with an interception that gave the Tigers their winning cushion.

There's Marquise Hill, another cat-quick defensive end, who made life miserable for the guys in red all evening long, knocking down passes and drilling ball carriers.

And there are those tireless speedsters in the secondary, Randall Gay and Eric Alexander and Corey Webster and Travis Daniels, who are either going for the quarterback's jugular or are running downfield tossing blankets on receivers.

Finally, there was Justin Vincent, whose 117 rushing yards made him the game's MVP, just as his 201 yards against Georgia made him the MVP of the SEC championship.

The case can be made that LSU kept the Sooners in the game, first with a penalty that erased a field goal that would have put the Tigers up by 17 in the third quarter, later with an interception of an errant throw by Matt Mauck that set up the seven

...that pulled the Sooners to within a touchdown.

It was fitting that Nick Saban's Tigers won a national championship with one defensive stop after another, a tribute to the architect who has made defense a mission, who has developed a disciplined consistency that has carried his ballclub to the heights all teams dream about.

Consider this: Saban's defense held a team that averaged 461 yards over the season to 154 yards — 52 yards of it rushing. LSU limited a team that averaged 45 points to a couple of touchdowns, one on a four-yard drive after a blocked punt, another on a 30-yard push following an

See FINNEY, A-7

JAN. 5, 2004